1,001 FACTS ABOUT HITTERS

D1049339

Nomar
Garciaparra

Mark
McGwire

Hank Aaron

Vladimir
Guerrero

MAJOR LEAGUE BASEBALL

1,001 *FACTS ABOUT*
HITTERS

*Mickey
Mantle*

By James Buckley, Jr.
Statistics Section Compiled By Matt Marini

DK Publishing, Inc.

LONDON, NEW YORK, MELBOURNE,
MUNICH, AND DELHI

Senior Editor Beth Sutinis
Senior Art Editor Michelle Baxter
Publisher Chuck Lang
Creative Director Tina Vaughan
Production Chris Avgherinos

Produced by
Shoreline Publishing Group LLC
Editorial Director James Buckley, Jr.
Art Director Tom Carling, Carling Design, Inc.

Produced in partnership and licensed by Major League Baseball Properties, Inc.
Vice President of Publishing Don Hintze

First American Edition, 2004
04 05 06 07 08 10 9 8 7 6 5 4 3 2 1

Published in the United States by DK Publishing, Inc.
375 Hudson Street, New York, New York 10014

A catalog record for this book is available from the Library of Congress.

ISBN: 0-7566-0494-X

DK Publishing books are available at special discounts for bulk purchases for sales promotions or premiums.
Special editions, including personalized covers, excerpts of existing guides, and corporate imprints can be
created in large quantities for specific needs. For more information, contact Special Markets Dept./
DK Publishing, Inc./375 Hudson Street/New York, New York 10014/FAX: 800-600-9098.

Color reproduction by Colourscan, Singapore
Printed in Singapore by Star Standard

Discover more at
www.dk.com

Contents

Ted Williams

Answers to trivia questions
can be found on page 168

Above Average

HITTING HAS BEEN CALLED
THE HARDEST THING
TO DO IN SPORTS.
MEET THE MEN WHO
DO A HARD JOB WELL.

Mike Piazza's .319 career batting average is second all-time among catchers in Major League history!

Wade Boggs

POSITION: Third base   **MLB CAREER: 1982–1999**

Wade Boggs proves that good things come to those who wait. First, Wade waited through six minor league seasons before making his big-league debut. He was an immediate hit, in more ways than one. After hitting .349 as a rookie in 1982, Wade won five of the next six A.L. batting titles. His patient lefthanded swing helped him become the first player to rack up more than 200 hits in seven straight seasons (1983–1989). In 1986, he helped the Red Sox reach the World Series, but they lost to the Mets.

His wait for a ring was soon, over however. After joining the Yankees in 1993, he helped them win the 1996 World Series. In 1999, with Tampa Bay, Wade got his 3,000th hit.

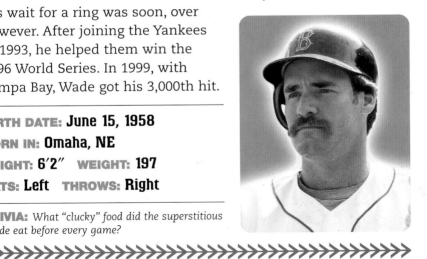

BIRTH DATE: June 15, 1958
BORN IN: Omaha, NE
HEIGHT: 6'2"   WEIGHT: 197
BATS: Left   THROWS: Right

TRIVIA: *What "clucky" food did the superstitious Wade eat before every game?*

>>

Rod Carew

POSITION: First/second base   **MLB CAREER: 1967–1985**

Rod Carew was born in Panama on a moving train, and he has rarely stopped moving since. Soon after Rod joined the Twins in 1967, pitchers discovered that he waved his bat "like a magic wand." Beginning in 1969, this hitting magician started a 15-season streak of hitting above .300. His career high was .388 in 1977, good for the sixth of his seven A.L. batting titles. Rod was also the A.L. MVP that season. Once on the basepaths with his many hits (he had 3,053 in his career), Rod was also a threat. He had seven seasons with at least 23 steals and tied a record with seven steals of home in 1969. In 1991, his career train made a stop at the Hall of Fame.

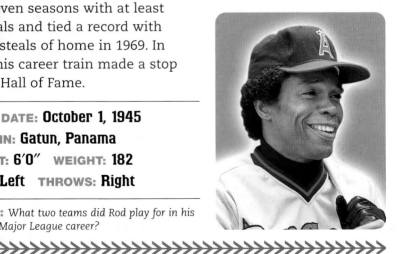

BIRTH DATE: October 1, 1945
BORN IN: Gatun, Panama
HEIGHT: 6′0″   **WEIGHT: 182**
BATS: Left   **THROWS: Right**

TRIVIA: *What two teams did Rod play for in his 19-year Major League career?*

Roberto Clemente

POSITION: Outfield   **MLB CAREER: 1955–1972**

Few players in baseball history have been as multitalented or have had such a lasting impact as Roberto Clemente. Roberto was one of the first players from Latin America to succeed in the Major Leagues. His great batting skills (.317 career average, including four N.L. batting titles) and incredible throwing arm (12 Gold Gloves, a record for outfielders) made him an awesome all-around player. He helped the Pirates win two World Series (1960 and 1971) and was the MVP of the '71 Series. But it was Roberto's contributions in the community—and his leadership in the Hispanic baseball world—that made him a real star. Today, baseball's highest service award is named for him.

BIRTH DATE: August 18, 1934
BORN IN: Carolina, Puerto Rico
HEIGHT: 5′11″   **WEIGHT: 175**
BATS: Right   **THROWS: Right**

TRIVIA: *Roberto grew up in Puerto Rico. What is the capital of that island commonwealth?*

Joe DiMaggio

POSITION: Outfield   **MLB CAREER: 1936–1951**

Joe DiMaggio had two famous nicknames, and both were accurate descriptions of his wonderful talents. "The Yankee Clipper" was a smooth, graceful fielder with a sweet, high-average swing that led to 11 .300-plus seasons (his career best was a league-leading .381 in 1939). "Joltin' Joe" had nine seasons with more than 100 RBI and seven 30-homer seasons (his best both came in 1937: 167 RBI and 46 dingers). But even with those great nicknames, Joe is best remembered for a number: 56. His

56-game hitting streak in 1941 is far and away the longest ever; no one has come within even 10 games of it since. He won three A.L. MVP awards, too.

BIRTH DATE: November 25, 1914
BORN IN: Martinez, CA
HEIGHT: 6′2″   WEIGHT: 193
BATS: Right   THROWS: Right

TRIVIA: *Can you name the two other DiMaggio brothers who played in the Majors?*

>>>

Vladimir Guerrero

POSITION: Outfield   **MLB CAREER: 1996–**

The Montreal Expos knew a good thing when they saw it. They signed Vladimir at the age of 16 after seeing him play only once. He was *that* good. Vladimir has since become one of the top all-around players in the game. In 2002, he led the N.L. with 206 hits, setting a team record. He also became one of only five players ever with five consecutive seasons with an average above .300 and at least 30 homers, 100 runs, and 100 RBI. Since batting .302 in 1997, his first full season, he has racked up seven straight

seasons with an average above .300. Vladimir also has one of the most feared throwing arms in the majors. In seven seasons, he has reached double figures in assists.

BIRTH DATE: February 9, 1976
BORN IN: Dominican Republic
HEIGHT: 6'3"   WEIGHT: 210
BATS: Right   THROWS: Right

TRIVIA: *The Montreal Expos are the only team to have its games broadcast in what language?*

Tony Gwynn

POSITION: Outfield   **MLB CAREER: 1982–2001**

To understand just how good a hitter Tony Gwynn was, consider this: Of the top 20 career hitters of all time, only Tony played after 1960. His .338 career mark is the best of the past 40 years! Tony tied a record set by the great Honus Wagner (page 98) with eight N.L. batting titles. He also had an amazing 19 straight seasons batting above .300, and was named to 15 All-Star Games. He wasn't just a great hitter, either. He earned five Gold Gloves for his defensive play and stole 319 bases, including

56 in 1987. In 1994, Tony found himself in elite company; his .394 average was the highest since Ted Williams hit .406 (see page 112) in 1941.

BIRTH DATE: May 9, 1960
BORN IN: Los Angeles, CA
HEIGHT: 5′11″   **WEIGHT: 199**
BATS: Left   **THROWS: Left**

TRIVIA: *In what two years did Tony help the San Diego Padres reach the World Series?*

>>>

Derek Jeter

POSITION: Shortstop **MLB CAREER: 1995–**

Although he won't turn 30 until 2004, Derek Jeter has already had a lifetime of baseball highlights. In high school in Michigan, he was named the national player of the year. In 1994, he was the minor league player of the year. And in 1996, as the first rookie starting shortstop for the Yankees in four years, he was the A.L. Rookie of the Year. To top it off, he has gone on to win four World Series rings with the Yankees and was the MVP of the 2000 Series. At the plate, Derek has batted above .300 six

times and scored more than 100 runs each year from 1996 to 2002. Though he's clutch at the plate, on the bases, and in the field, Derek's best role is as a team leader.

BIRTH DATE: June 26, 1974
BORN IN: Pequannock, NJ
HEIGHT: 6'3" **WEIGHT: 195**
BATS: Right **THROWS: Right**

TRIVIA: *What "neighborly" team did Derek help the Yankees defeat in the 2000 World Series?*

Stan Musial

POSITION: Outfield   MLB CAREER: 1941–1963

The luckiest fall in Cardinals' history came in 1940. A young player ticketed to be a lefthanded pitcher fell while playing outfield and hurt his pitching shoulder. After switching to the outfield fulltime, that kid became "The Man." Stan Musial finished his Hall of Fame career with an N.L.-best 3,630 hits and a .331 average. He won three MVP awards and seven N.L. batting titles, but he was no singles hitter. "Stan the Man" had 475 career homers and led the league in slugging percentage six times. He set a record with five homers in a doubleheader. Stan, who was named to 24 All-Star teams, helped St. Louis win four N.L. titles and three World Series titles (1942, '44, and '46.)

BIRTH DATE: November 21, 1920
BORN IN: Donora, PA
HEIGHT: 6′0″   WEIGHT: 175
BATS: Left   THROWS: Left

TRIVIA: *What was the name of the other St. Louis team that Stan faced in the 1944 Series?*

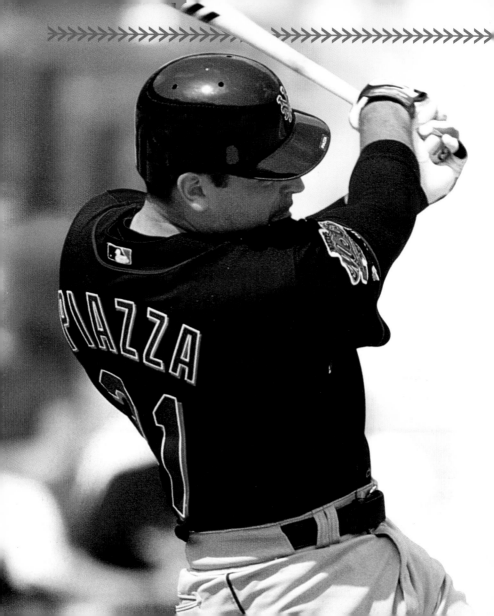

Mike Piazza

POSITION: Catcher   **MLB CAREER: 1992–**

To put it simply, Mike Piazza is the greatest hitting catcher in baseball history. Mike has come a long way from being selected in the 62nd round of the 1988 amateur draft. He worked hard in the minors and quickly established himself as a high-average slugger. He was the 1993 N.L. Rookie of the Year, the 1996 All-Star Game MVP, and finished second in the N.L. MVP race in 1996 and 1997. In '97, he set a record for catchers with 195 hits. Mike's 10 Silver Slugger awards (given to the best hitter at each position) are a record for catchers, as are his 10 straight seasons with 20 or more homers. His .319 career batting average is second highest all-time among catchers, too.

BIRTH DATE: September 4, 1968
BORN IN: Norristown, PA
HEIGHT: 6′3″   WEIGHT: 215
BATS: Right   THROWS: Right

TRIVIA: *Heading into 2004, what player did Mike trail on the catchers' career homer list?*

>>

Albert Pujols

POSITION: **Outfield**   MLB CAREER: **2001–**

Talk about your fast starts! In 2003, Albert Pujols became the first player in Major League history to have at least 30 homers, 100 RBI, and 100 runs in his first three seasons. He also finished in the top five in N.L. MVP voting each year, too. He capped off his first trio of pro seasons by winning the N.L. batting title in 2003 with a huge .359 average. Albert burst into the Majors in 2001 with one of the best rookie seasons ever (.329 average, 37 homers, 130 RBI). He also had enough versatility to

play first base, third base, and the outfield. Albert's skill at the plate amazes his veteran teammates. "He just always seems to hit the ball really hard," says Jim Edmonds.

BIRTH DATE: **January 16, 1980**
BORN IN: **Dominican Republic**
HEIGHT: **6′2″**   WEIGHT: **210**
BATS: **Right**   THROWS: **Right**

TRIVIA: *What is the home ballpark for Albert's St. Louis Cardinals team?*

>>

Pete Rose

POSITION: OF, 1B, 2B, 3B   **MLB CAREER: 1963–1986**

Pete Rose played like that bunny in the battery commercial. No matter what position he played for what team, he just kept on hitting and hitting and hitting.... In 1985, the man they called "Charlie Hustle" for his all-out style of play, broke a record many thought could never be broken. With a solid single to left field, Pete became baseball's all-time leader in hits, knocking Ty Cobb (page 88) out of the top spot. When Pete finally stopped, he had 4,256 hits. Now, of course, everyone says that record will never be

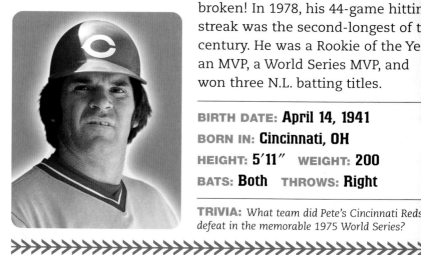

broken! In 1978, his 44-game hitting streak was the second-longest of the century. He was a Rookie of the Year, an MVP, a World Series MVP, and won three N.L. batting titles.

BIRTH DATE: April 14, 1941
BORN IN: Cincinnati, OH
HEIGHT: 5'11"   **WEIGHT: 200**
BATS: Both   **THROWS: Right**

TRIVIA: *What team did Pete's Cincinnati Reds defeat in the memorable 1975 World Series?*

Home Run Heroes

GOING, GOING, GONE!
THE HOME RUN IS THE
GAME'S MOST EXCITING
PLAY. MEET THE MEN WHO
"WENT YARD."

Babe Ruth put the home run on the baseball map, retiring with a then-record 714 career homers.

Hank Aaron

POSITION: Outfield   **MLB CAREER:** 1954–1976

Hank Aaron comes first alphabetically on the list of all Major League players. He also comes first on the list of home run kings. "Hammerin' Hank" thrilled most of the nation in 1974 when he hit his record-breaking 715th home run. Hank courageously faced down racists who didn't want to see him break Babe Ruth's record. But anyone who had to pitch against this 21-time All-Star knew it was just a matter of time. His quick wrists and smooth swing turned into 755 career homers as well as an all-time record 2,297 RBI. He had at least 30 homers every season but one from 1957 (when he helped the Braves win the World Series) to 1971, plus 14 .300-plus seasons.

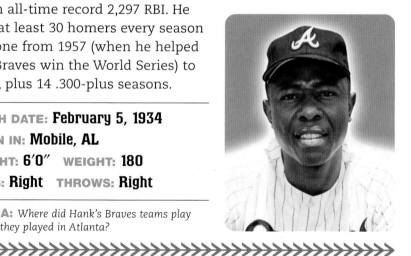

BIRTH DATE: February 5, 1934
BORN IN: Mobile, AL
HEIGHT: 6'0"   **WEIGHT:** 180
BATS: Right   **THROWS:** Right

TRIVIA: Where did Hank's Braves teams play before they played in Atlanta?

>>>

Ernie Banks

POSITION: **Shortstop, 1B**   MLB CAREER: **1953–1971**

Few players have loved playing baseball more than Ernie Banks. One reason he loved it, of course, was that he was one of the best of his time. Ernie was one of the first shortstops with real power, as his 512 lifetime homers show. He later moved to first base and continued his slugging ways, racking up eight career 100-RBI seasons. Though he played for Cubs' teams that had little success, his greatness was recognized with two MVP awards (1958 and 1959). Ernie's love of the game is best shown with his famous remark, "It's a beautiful day for baseball. Let's play two." The 11-time All-Star they called "Mr. Cub" was named to the Hall of Fame in 1977.

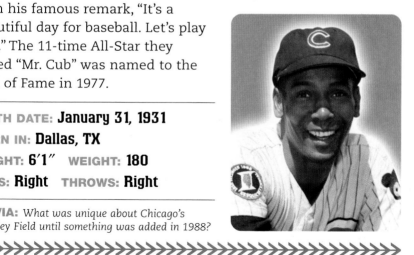

BIRTH DATE: **January 31, 1931**
BORN IN: **Dallas, TX**
HEIGHT: **6'1"**   WEIGHT: **180**
BATS: **Right**   THROWS: **Right**

TRIVIA: *What was unique about Chicago's Wrigley Field until something was added in 1988?*

>>>

Barry Bonds

POSITION: **Outfield**   **MLB CAREER:** **1986–**

Barry Bonds just might be the greatest all-around player in baseball history. He was certainly the best player in the 1990s, winning three of his record six career MVP awards in the decade, along with eight Gold Gloves. After that amazing decade, incredibly, in the 2000s, he got even better! Barry's greatest season came in 2001. As the country watched every at-bat, he cracked an all-time record 73 homers. Barry followed that up in 2002 by winning his first batting title (.370 at the age of 38!) and

leading the Giants to the World Series, smashing a record eight homers in the postseason. In 2002, he became only the fourth player to top 600 career homers.

BIRTH DATE: **July 24, 1964**
BORN IN: **Riverside, CA**
HEIGHT: **6'2"**   **WEIGHT:** **230**
BATS: **Left**   **THROWS:** **Left**

TRIVIA: *What team did Barry play for before joining the Giants in 1993?*

≫≫≫≫≫≫≫≫≫≫≫≫≫≫≫≫≫≫≫≫≫≫≫≫≫≫≫≫

Josh Gibson

POSITION: **Catcher**   CAREER: **1929–1946**

Because he was African-American, Josh Gibson was not allowed to play in the Majors. However, some experts say he might have been the greatest home run hitter of all time. Josh starred in the Negro Leagues, which were created to give black players a place to play pro baseball. Statistics back then weren't official, but some of Gibson's reported numbers are stunning: 75 homers in 1931; a batting average of .393 in 1945; a career total of nearly 800 home runs. Josh was extremely strong, with an ability to simply crush the ball. He had a super throwing arm from behind the plate. Though he never made it to the Majors, Josh made it to the Hall of Fame in 1972.

BIRTH DATE: **December 21, 1911**
BORN IN: **Buena Vista, GA**
HEIGHT: **6′1″**   WEIGHT: **210**
BATS: **Right**   THROWS: **Right**

TRIVIA: *What team, on which Josh starred, do many consider the best Negro League team ever?*

>>

Ken Griffey, Jr.

POSITION: Outfield **MLB CAREER:** 1989–

You can't say this about too many players: He is the complete package. The experts call them "five-tool" players, and Ken Griffey, Jr., is a master with all five tools. Hit for power? He has seven seasons with 40 or more homers and is a four-time A.L. home run champ. Hit for average? Six seasons with an average above .300. Glove and arm? Ten straight Gold Gloves and a reputation as the best outfielder in the game. Speed? He's no Rickey Henderson, but he has 10 seasons with double-digit steals. In 1999, Ken was the youngest player named to the All-Century team. Injuries have slowed this superstar in recent years, but "Junior" is still one of the great ones.

BIRTH DATE: November 21, 1969
BORN IN: Donora, PA
HEIGHT: 6'3"   **WEIGHT:** 205
BATS: Left   **THROWS:** Left

TRIVIA: *With what team did Ken's father, Ken, Sr., win World Series titles in 1975 and 1976?*

Reggie Jackson

POSITION: Outfield   **MLB CAREER: 1967–1987**

On baseball's biggest stage, Reggie Jackson shone brightest. In the 1977 World Series, Reggie, already a huge star, cemented his Hall of Fame status by smacking three homers on three straight pitches. The blasts helped the Yankees beat the Dodgers and secure another World Series title. Reggie had already slugged the Oakland A's to three straight Series titles (1972–1974); he was the A.L. MVP in 1973. Moving to the Yankees, he continued his winning ways, helping the Bronx Bombers win it all in 1977 and

1978. In 27 total World Series games, Reggie had 10 homers and 24 RBI, along with eight dingers in other playoff action. This superstar joined the Hall of Fame in 1993.

BIRTH DATE: May 18, 1946
BORN IN: Wyncote, PA
HEIGHT: 6'0"   **WEIGHT: 200**
BATS: Left   **THROWS: Left**

TRIVIA: *What unusual baseball-themed treat was named for this slugger?*

〉〉〉

Willie Mays

POSITION: **Outfield**   MLB CAREER: **1951–1973**

Willie Mays' famous nickname was "The Say Hey Kid." But all anyone who saw him play could do was "Say Wow!" Willie was one of the greatest power hitters ever; his 660 home runs are third all-time. He was also one of the game's greatest fielders. Along with 12 Gold Gloves (tied for most among outfielders), he is the all-time leader in outfield putouts. In 1954, he made what many call the greatest play ever, "The Catch" in the World Series. In various years, he led the N.L. in stolen bases, triples, walks, homers, and slugging percentage. He also played in a record 24 All-Star Games, setting numerous records. Willie was a two-time N.L. MVP and joined the Hall of Fame in 1979.

BIRTH DATE: **May 6, 1931**
BORN IN: **Westfield, AL**
HEIGHT: **5'11"**   WEIGHT: **180**
BATS: **Right**   THROWS: **Right**

TRIVIA: *Willie played for the Giants in two different cities: Can you name them?*

Mark McGwire

POSITION: First base **MLB CAREER: 1986–2001**

Big Mac could smack! Mark McGwire already had been a top power hitter for more than a decade (since he belted a rookie record 49 homers in 1987) when he became not just one of the greatest homer-hitters ever, but also an American folk hero. His stunning 1998 season saw him become the first player ever to hit 70 homers, watched eagerly by baseball-loving fans. It was part of a run in which he became the first player with four straight 50-homer seasons (1996–1999). His 135 homers in 1998–1999 count as the highest two-season total ever. He ended his career sixth all-time with 583 home runs and was named one of two first basemen on the 1999 All-Century Team.

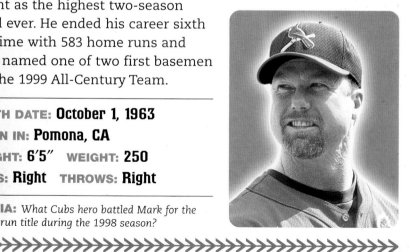

BIRTH DATE: October 1, 1963

BORN IN: Pomona, CA

HEIGHT: 6′5″ **WEIGHT: 250**

BATS: Right **THROWS: Right**

TRIVIA: *What Cubs hero battled Mark for the home run title during the 1998 season?*

>>>

Rafael Palmeiro

POSITION: First base/DH **MLB CAREER: 1986–**

Rafael Palmeiro might be called a quiet superstar. After many seasons of solid play, Rafael suddenly caught fans' attention in 2003 when he hit his 500th career home run. He was only the 19th player ever, and the first Cuban-born player, to reach that historic mark. Steady success is his trademark. In 2003, "Raffy" extended his Major League record with his ninth straight season with at least 38 homers; Babe Ruth is second with seven such seasons. Rafael was second among all players in hits in the 1990s, and is second overall in total RBI since 1990. Best of all for his teams, he never seems to miss a game: Only twice from 1988 to 2003 did he play in fewer than 152 games.

BIRTH DATE: September 24, 1964
BORN IN: Havana, Cuba
HEIGHT: 6'0" **WEIGHT: 188**
BATS: Left **THROWS: Left**

TRIVIA: *Where did the Rangers' team play before moving to Texas in 1972?*

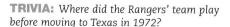

Alex Rodriguez

POSITION: **Shortstop**   MLB CAREER: **1994–**

Until Alex "A-Rod" Rodriguez came along, shortstops were expected to be great fielders, and if they hit…it was a bonus. There were a few slugging shortstops, such as Cubs great Ernie Banks (page 34), but then along came A-Rod to set a new standard. The first player chosen in the 1993 amateur draft, he was the 1996 Rookie of the Year and finished second in the A.L. MVP voting after winning the league batting title with a .358 average. He continues to hit for a good average (five more

.300 seasons), but is making his biggest mark with homers. In 2003, A-Rod's all-around skills finally earned him the A.L. MVP award.

BIRTH DATE: **July 27, 1975**
BORN IN: **New York, NY**
HEIGHT: **6'3"**   WEIGHT: **210**
BATS: **Right**   THROWS: **Right**

TRIVIA: *Alex's 57 homers in 2002 were the most in the A.L. since what famous slugger in 1961?*

>>>

Babe Ruth

POSITION: **Outfield**   **MLB CAREER:** **1914–1935**

George Herman "Babe" Ruth was simply the greatest baseball player of all time. He started as a pitcher and became one of the best of his time, setting a record for consecutive scoreless innings in the World Series that stood for more than 40 years. As a hitter, he was the ultimate slugger. When entire teams were hitting 20 or 30 homers a season, Ruth himself was hitting more than 50. He led the A.L. 12 times and 11 times topped 40 homers in a season. His .690 career slugging average is a record. He was the first to hit 60 homers in a season (1927) and was the career leader with 714 until topped by Hank Aaron. Babe is still the player against whom all great players are judged.

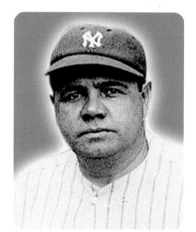

BIRTH DATE: **February 6, 1895**
BORN IN: **Baltimore, MD**
HEIGHT: **6′2″**   **WEIGHT:** **215**
BATS: **Left**   **THROWS:** **Left**

TRIVIA: *For what team did Babe pitch in World Series in 1916 and 1918?*

Mike Schmidt

POSITION: Third base **MLB CAREER: 1972–1989**

Want to know how big a slugger Mike Schmidt was? Only Babe Ruth led his league in homers more times than Mike's eight N.L. home run titles. That's pretty good company, but with 548 lifetime dingers, this Phillies great is used to it. He was more than a slugger, however. His 10 Gold Gloves are second among third basemen behind Brooks Robinson. Mike was a three-time N.L. MVP and a 12-time All-Star selection while anchoring the Phillies' lineup for 18 seasons. On April 17, 1976, Mike joined an

elite group of hitters who have hit four homers in a single game. In 1980, he helped the Phillies win their first World Series. Mike slugged his way into the Hall of Fame in 1995.

BIRTH DATE: September 27, 1949
BORN IN: Dayton, OH
HEIGHT: 6′2″ WEIGHT: 203
BATS: Right   THROWS: Right

TRIVIA: *What A.L. team did Mike and the Phillies beat to win the 1980 World Series?*

>>

Sammy Sosa

POSITION: Outfield   **MLB CAREER: 1989–**

For the first part of his career, Sammy Sosa was a slugging outfielder with some speed and a great throwing arm. Then, almost from nowhere, in 1998, he became one of the game's greatest all-time sluggers. His epic duel that summer with Mark McGwire, as both players chased Roger Maris' record of 61 homers, thrilled the nation's fans. Though McGwire set the record with 70 (since topped by Barry Bonds with 73), Sammy's buoyant personality and powerful swing made him a hero. He

has since become the only player with three 60-homer seasons and one of only three with nine straight 35-homer, 100-RBI years. In 2003, he joined the 500-career-homer club!

BIRTH DATE: November 12, 1968
BORN IN: Dominican Republic
HEIGHT: 6'0"   **WEIGHT: 185**
BATS: Right   **THROWS: Right**

TRIVIA: *What is the fan-friendly home park of Sammy and the Chicago Cubs?*

>>

Jim Thome

POSITION: First base   **MLB CAREER: 1991–**

Over the past 10 years, Jim Thome has been among baseball's best and most consistent power hitters. In 1999, Jim was part of a powerful Indians lineup that became the first team since 1950 to score more than 1,000 runs in a season; Jim drove in 108 of them. Jim helped the Indians win five straight A.L. Central titles (1995–1999). With Cleveland, he had a team-record seven straight 30-homer seasons, including a club-record 52 in 2002, along with six years with more than 100 RBI. After joining Philadelphia for the 2003 season, Jim just kept slugging, ending the year with 47 homers (tops in the N.L.) and 131 RBI. Jim started as a third baseman, moving to first in 1997.

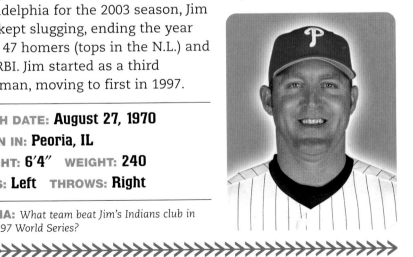

BIRTH DATE: August 27, 1970
BORN IN: Peoria, IL
HEIGHT: 6′4″   WEIGHT: 240
BATS: Left   THROWS: Right

TRIVIA: *What team beat Jim's Indians club in the 1997 World Series?*

>>>>>>>>>>>>>>>>>>>>>>>>>>>>>>>>>>>>>>>

RBI Men

YOUR TEAM CAN'T WIN
IF YOU DON'T SCORE.
THESE ARE THE PLAYERS
WHO EXCELLED AT
DRIVING IN RUNS.

Toronto's slugging first baseman Carlos Delgado led the Major Leagues with 145 RBI in 2003.

Jeff Bagwell

POSITION: First base   **MLB CAREER:** 1991–

Every time Jeff Bagwell smacks another homer, fans in Boston cringe. The Red Sox traded young rookie Jeff to the Houston Astros in 1990 and have watched him blossom into one of baseball's most consistent run-producers. Since joining the Astros, Jeff has racked up nine seasons of 30-plus homers (an Astros record) and has eight 100-RBI seasons. He was the 1994 N.L. MVP. Though he came up in the minors as a third baseman, he switched to first with Houston and improved quickly enough

to win a Gold Glove. "Bags" has one of baseball's oddest batting stances—spreading his feet very wide and crouching—but he makes it work.

BIRTH DATE: May 27, 1968
BORN IN: Boston, MA
HEIGHT: 6'0" **WEIGHT:** 215
BATS: Right **THROWS:** Right

TRIVIA: *What was the famous "indoor" home of the Astros from 1965 through 1999?*

≫≫≫≫≫≫≫≫≫≫≫≫≫≫≫≫≫≫≫≫≫≫≫≫≫≫≫≫≫≫≫≫

Johnny Bench

POSITION: Catcher **MLB CAREER:** 1967–1983

Johnny Bench was one of only two catchers named to the All-Century Team in 1999. But although he won 10 Gold Gloves and was one of the first catchers to use a one-handed catching style with a hinged mitt, he knew his place. "My job on the Reds is to drive in runs," he once said. He sure succeeded, with six 100-RBI seasons, including three times leading the N.L. His great all-around play helped him win just about every award possible: 1968 N.L. Rookie of the Year, 1970 and 1972 N.L. MVP, 1976 World Series MVP. Before Mike Piazza (page 24) came along, Johnny was arguably the best-hitting catcher in baseball history. He joined the greats in the Hall of Fame in 1989.

BIRTH DATE: December 7, 1947
BORN IN: Oklahoma City, OK
HEIGHT: 6′1″ **WEIGHT:** 208
BATS: Right **THROWS:** Right

TRIVIA: *What was the nickname of the Reds' team that won the 1975 and 1976 World Series?*

>>>

Yogi Berra

POSITION: Catcher, OF   **MLB CAREER: 1946–1965**

As the Yankees dominated the A.L. in the 1950s, Yogi Berra was a key part of the team, winning three A.L. MVP awards (1951, '54, and '55). Though he played the demanding position of catcher, he was an offensive threat, with five 100-RBI seasons in the decade. Also, no player appeared in more World Series than Yogi. He played on a record 10 world championship clubs and holds career World Series records for hits and games played. Along with his great baseball skills, Yogi is well known for his unusual sayings, such as "It ain't over 'til it's over." Yogi was named to the Hall of Fame in 1972 and was one of only two catchers named to the All-Century Team in 1999.

BIRTH DATE: May 12, 1925
BORN IN: St. Louis, MO
HEIGHT: 5′8″   WEIGHT: 194
BATS: Left   THROWS: Right

TRIVIA: *What famous cartoon character was named for this Hall of Fame catcher?*

Carlos Delgado

POSITION: First base   **MLB CAREER: 1993–**

Since he became Toronto's regular first baseman in 1996, Carlos Delgado has been the man the Blue Jays turn to when they need a big hit. He has had at least 90 RBI in each of the past eight seasons, and has topped 100 in six of those years. His 137 RBI in 2000 helped him win the Hank Aaron Award as the A.L.'s top offensive player. In 2003, he led the Majors with 145 RBI. Part of his success comes through the long ball, with seven straight 30-homer seasons, beginning with 30 in 1997 and topped by 44 in 1999. On September 25, 2003, Carlos became only the fifteenth Major League player to slug four homers in one game! He did it in four straight at-bats against Tampa Bay.

BIRTH DATE: June 25, 1972
BORN IN: Aguadilla, Puerto Rico
HEIGHT: 6′3″   WEIGHT: 230
BATS: Right   THROWS: Right

TRIVIA: *In what year did the Toronto Blue Jays play their first game?*

Nomar Garciaparra

POSITION: Shortstop   **MLB CAREER: 1996–**

Nomar is the latest in a long line of clutch Red Sox hitters. After a "cup of coffee" (a few games) with Boston in 1996, he burst onto the scene in 1997 with 98 RBI as a rookie, while batting .306 and winning A.L. Rookie of the Year honors. He has become the Red Sox go-to guy every season since, playing with fiery intensity and acting as a team leader. While helping Boston reach the playoffs four times, Nomar has had more than 96 RBI in six seasons. He also led the A.L. in batting in 1999 and 2000, while continuing his great defensive play, too. Before joining the Red Sox organization, Nomar attended Georgia Tech University and played for the U.S. team at the 1992 Olympic Games.

BIRTH DATE: July 23, 1973
BORN IN: Whittier, CA
HEIGHT: 6'0"   WEIGHT: 185
BATS: Right   THROWS: Right

NOMAR TRIVIA: *How did Nomar get his name? Hint: His dad's name is Ramon.*

Jason Giambi

POSITION: First base **MLB CAREER:** 1995–

Jason Giambi spends hours practicing hitting, whacking a ball off a tee, taking time in the cage, and working out. All that hard work pays off with tons of RBI for his teams. Jason has six seasons with more than 100 RBI. His career high of 137 RBI (and 43 homers) came in Oakland during 2000, when he was named the A.L. MVP. He proved his all-around hitting when he batted a career-high .342 the next year. After joining the Yankees in 2002, he kept things rolling with more than 40 homers and 100 RBI in

each of his first two seasons in New York. Though he has already put up some great numbers, look for even bigger things from this slugger in the years to come.

BIRTH DATE: January 8, 1971
BORN IN: West Covina, CA
HEIGHT: 6′2″ **WEIGHT:** 235
BATS: Left **THROWS:** Right

TRIVIA: *What famous Yankees nickname includes the part of New York they play in?*

≫≫≫≫≫≫≫≫≫≫≫≫≫≫≫≫≫≫≫≫≫≫≫≫≫≫≫≫≫

Juan Gonzalez

POSITION: Outfield   **MLB CAREER: 1989–**

Juan Gonzalez is an RBI man of historic proportion. In 1998, his 157 RBI were the most by an A.L. player since Boston's Ted Williams and Vern Stephens had 159…in 1949! Juan won his second A.L. MVP award for that outstanding feat. Since becoming a regular in the Texas outfield in 1991, Juan has been one of baseball's steadiest run-producers, with eight seasons of more than 100 RBI. Texas sure loves Juan; he is the team's all-time leader in homers, RBI, and total bases. Plus, he has led the team

to its only four division championships. He has five seasons with more than 40 homers, and in 2002, he became the 34th player ever with more than 400 career homers.

BIRTH DATE: October 20, 1969
BORN IN: Arecibo, Puerto Rico
HEIGHT: 6'3"   **WEIGHT: 210**
BATS: Right   **THROWS: Right**

TRIVIA: *When Juan won the 1998 A.L. MVP, what slugger from Chicago won the N.L. award?*

Hank Greenberg

POSITION: First base   **MLB CAREER: 1930–1947**

Hank Greenberg's lifetime stats earned him a well-deserved spot in the Hall of Fame. But his numbers would have been better had he not spent four prime years of his career serving his country. The A.L. MVP in 1935 (when he helped Detroit win the World Series) as well as in 1940, he also slugged 183 RBI in 1937 and nearly matched Babe Ruth by hitting 58 homers in 1938. Yet he left the game behind in 1941 to join the Army before World War II started. He returned to the field in 1945, helped lead the

Tigers to another world title, and then led the A.L. in homers and RBI in 1946. As one of the earliest Jewish ballplayers, Hank was a hero to many youngsters.

BIRTH DATE: January 1, 1911
BORN IN: New York, NY
HEIGHT: 6′3″   **WEIGHT: 210**
BATS: Right   **THROWS: Right**

TRIVIA: *When was the last time the Detroit Tigers won the World Series?*

⫸⫸⫸⫸⫸⫸⫸⫸⫸⫸⫸⫸⫸⫸⫸⫸⫸⫸⫸⫸⫸⫸⫸⫸⫸⫸⫸⫸

Jeff Kent

POSITION: **Second base**   **MLB CAREER:** **1992–**

Very few second basemen have been as productive at the plate as Jeff Kent. He spent his first five seasons with the Mets, Blue Jays, and Indians. Jeff really blossomed after he joined the Giants in 1997. With 121 RBI that year and 128 the next, he became only the second second baseman ever with consecutive 120-RBI years (the first was Hall of Famer Rogers Hornsby, page 106). He followed those years with four more 100-RBI campaigns. His best year was 2000, in which he hit 33 homers, had 125 RBI, and finished with a career-best .334 average. While helping the Giants to baseball's best record, Jeff became the first second baseman since 1984 to win the N.L. MVP award.

BIRTH DATE: **March 7, 1968**
BORN IN: **Bellflower, CA**
HEIGHT: **6′1″**   **WEIGHT:** **215**
BATS: **Right**   **THROWS:** **Right**

TRIVIA: *What team did Jeff and the Giants face in the 2002 World Series?*

Manny Ramirez

POSITION: **Outfield** MLB CAREER: **1993–**

No matter where he plays, Manny Ramirez drives in runs in bunches. The former New York City high school phenom joined Cleveland in 1993 and moved to the Red Sox in 2001. Manny has eight 100-RBI seasons in his career, including six in a row from 1998 to 2003. That streak was highlighted by his league-leading 165 RBI with Cleveland in 1999 (which set a new team record) and 145 RBI in 1998. Manny also proved how complete a hitter he is by winning the A.L. batting title in 2002 with a .349 average. Only once in a full season has he batted below .306. You want power, too? Manny has eight seasons with 30 homers, including a career high 45 in 1998.

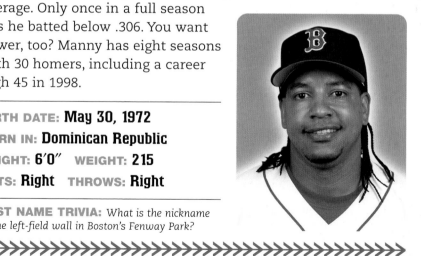

BIRTH DATE: **May 30, 1972**
BORN IN: **Dominican Republic**
HEIGHT: **6'0"** WEIGHT: **215**
BATS: **Right** THROWS: **Right**

LAST NAME TRIVIA: *What is the nickname of the left-field wall in Boston's Fenway Park?*

>>>

Hack Wilson

POSITION: Outfield   **MLB CAREER:** 1923–1934

For one season, Lewis Robert "Hack" Wilson was the greatest RBI man ever. In 1930, he drove in 191 runs for the Cubs. It was the fourth season in a row he had at least 120 RBI. He set a new N.L. record with 56 home runs, a mark that would stand until Mark McGwire and Sammy Sosa surpassed it in 1998. Wilson did not look like a typical ballplayer. He was shorter than most players, but he boasted enormous arms and powerful legs. His strength helped him lead the N.L. in homers four times. He

also batted above .300 five times, including an N.L.-best .356 in 1930. Some think he was called Hack because he looked like a wrestler named George Hackenschmidt.

BIRTH DATE: April 26, 1900
BORN IN: Ellwood City, PA
HEIGHT: 5'6"   **WEIGHT:** 190
BATS: Right   **THROWS:** Right

TRIVIA: *Hack's 191 RBI is the N.L. record for a season. Who holds the A.L. single-season mark?*

>>>

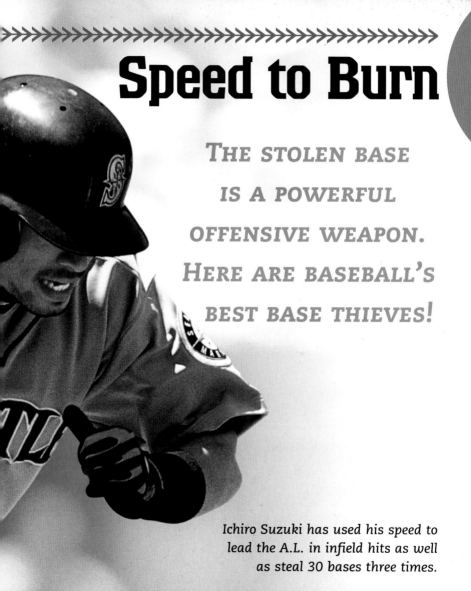

Speed to Burn

THE STOLEN BASE IS A POWERFUL OFFENSIVE WEAPON. HERE ARE BASEBALL'S BEST BASE THIEVES!

Ichiro Suzuki has used his speed to lead the A.L. in infield hits as well as steal 30 bases three times.

Lou Brock

POSITION: **Outfield** MLB CAREER: **1961–1979**

The Chicago Cubs' loss was the St. Louis Cardinals'—and baseball's—gain. In 1964, unheralded outfielder Lou Brock was sent to St. Louis from Chicago for pitcher Ernie Broglio. It's not surprising that the deal is considered a steal, since all Lou did in St. Louis was set a new modern record for career steals with 938, including a record 118 in 1974 (Rickey Henderson, page 90, has since broken both marks). To steal all those bases, Lou had to get on base. His lifetime .293 average helped him

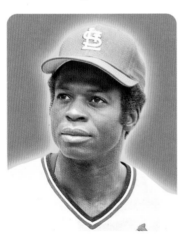

become, in 1979, the 13th player ever with 3,000 career hits. His game-changing speed and his all-around excellent play led him—on the fast track—to the Hall of Fame in 1985.

BIRTH DATE: **June 18, 1939**
BORN IN: **El Dorado, AR**
HEIGHT: **5′11″** WEIGHT: **170**
BATS: **Left** THROWS: **Left**

TRIVIA: *In what two years did Lou help the Cardinals win World Series championships?*

>>

Ty Cobb

POSITION: **Outfield**   MLB CAREER: **1905–1928**

On the short list of "greatest players ever," Ty Cobb's name must appear. Along with unmatched batting and running skills, Ty brought to his game a fierce competitiveness that made him among baseball's most feared opponents. Ty would do just about anything to win. In 1907, he won the first of his record 12 A.L. batting titles; he led the league in hits eight times on his way to a then-record 4,189 career hits. Once on base he was a terror, leading the league in stolen bases eight times. His career total of

892 was the modern record for more than 50 years. Ty's amazing accomplishments put him among the first group of players elected to the Hall of Fame in 1936.

BIRTH DATE: **December 18, 1886**
BORN IN: **Narrows, GA**
HEIGHT: **6'1"**   WEIGHT: **175**
BATS: **Left**   THROWS: **Right**

TRIVIA: *What was Ty's famous nickname, inspired by his birthplace?*

>>

Rickey Henderson

POSITION: **Outfield**   **MLB CAREER:** **1979–**

If the object of baseball is to score runs, then Rickey Henderson can be called the most successful player in history. In 2002, Rickey passed Ty Cobb as the all-time leader in runs scored. He also overtook Babe Ruth to become the career leader in walks. That's on top of the record he set in 1991, when he became the career leader in stolen bases. Rickey ended 2003 more than 400 steals ahead of Lou Brock. Rickey also holds the single-season record of 130 steals, set in 1982, and led the A.L. a record 12 times

in that category. Henderson's speed and ability to get on base (more than 3,000 career hits) makes him, without question, the best leadoff hitter ever to play the game.

BIRTH DATE: **December 25, 1958**
BORN IN: **Chicago, IL**
HEIGHT: **5'10"**   **WEIGHT:** **195**
BATS: **Right**   **THROWS:** **Left**

TRIVIA: *What year did Rickey win the A.L. MVP award while helping Oakland to the World Series?*

>>>

Jackie Robinson

POSITION: **Second base**   **MLB CAREER:** **1947–1956**

Few players can be said to have "changed the game." Even fewer people can say they changed America. Jackie Robinson did both. As the first African-American to play in the modern Major Leagues, at his debut in 1947, Jackie showed remarkable courage and inspired millions to work for further change in society. For baseball, however, he turned speed into an offensive weapon. His energetic baserunning—stealing, taking the extra base, daring offenses to stop him—unnerved opponents and thrilled fans. He helped the Brooklyn Dodgers to six N.L. pennants and the 1955 World Series championship. In 1997, Jackie's number 42 was retired by all Major League teams.

BIRTH DATE: **January 31, 1919**
BORN IN: **Cairo, GA**
HEIGHT: **5′11″**   **WEIGHT:** **204**
BATS: **Right**   **THROWS:** **Right**

TRIVIA: *What was the name of the Brooklyn Dodgers' famous home ballpark?*

➤➤➤➤➤➤➤➤➤➤➤➤➤➤➤➤➤➤➤➤➤➤➤➤➤➤➤➤➤➤➤➤➤➤➤➤

Ichiro Suzuki

POSITION: **Outfield**   **MLB CAREER:** **2001–**

Baseball experts debated whether Ichiro Suzuki, the first non-pitcher ever to jump from the Japanese pro league to the Majors, would succeed or fail. He succeeded—beyond everyone's wildest imagination! In his first year, he was the Rookie of the Year, the A.L. MVP, led the A.L. in batting and steals, and started the All-Star Game (with the most votes of any player). His 450 hits were the most ever by a player in his first two seasons, and his consecutive Gold Gloves are proof of what many say—that he is baseball's best rightfielder. Along with his phenomenal hitting ability, Ichiro is one of baseball's fastest players, with at least 30 steals in each of his three seasons.

BIRTH DATE: **November 22, 1973**
BORN IN: **Kasugai, Japan**
HEIGHT: **5′9″**   **WEIGHT:** **160**
BATS: **Left**   **THROWS:** **Right**

TRIVIA: *How many teams play in Japan's two pro leagues (Pacific and Central)?*

>>>

Alfonso Soriano

POSITION: Second base   MLB CAREER: **1999–**

With his blinding speed, young Dominican superstar Alfonso Soriano was expected to be a basestealing wizard. In his short career, that has proven to be true, as he has stolen at least 32 bases in each of his first three full seasons, with a career high of 43 in 2001. But what has surprised both teammates and opponents alike has been Alfonso's ability to combine power with speed. In 2002, he joined the 30-30 club (at least 30 steals and 30 homers in the same season), also coming within one

homer of becoming only the fourth player ever in the 40-40 club! In 2003, he did it again, proving that this double threat has earned a spot among baseball's best players.

BIRTH DATE: January 7, 1978
BORN IN: Dominican Republic
HEIGHT: 6'1"   WEIGHT: 180
BATS: Right   THROWS: Right

TRIVIA: *Can you name the three players who are members of the 40 homer/40 steal club?*

≫≫≫≫≫≫≫≫≫≫≫≫≫≫≫≫≫≫≫≫≫≫≫≫≫≫≫≫≫≫≫

Honus Wagner

POSITION: Shortstop   **MLB CAREER: 1897–1917**

Most of baseball's early stars have been eclipsed in some ways by modern players. However, along with Ty Cobb, the great shortstop Honus Wagner was the only position player from before World War I named to baseball's 1999 All-Century Team. Wagner remains one of baseball's greatest hitters, with eight N.L. batting titles and a .327 lifetime average. Along with being a baserunning star, leading the league in steals five times, Honus paced the N.L. in various years in runs, hits, doubles, RBI, triples,

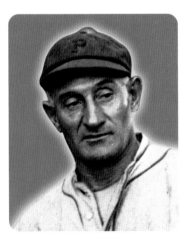

and slugging percentage. He was one of the game's best-loved people, too, and played shortstop with ferocity. He was one of the first five players named to the Hall of Fame in 1936.

BIRTH DATE: February 24, 1874
BORN IN: Chartiers, PA
HEIGHT: 5′11″   **WEIGHT: 200**
BATS: Right   **THROWS: Right**

TRIVIA: *In what year did Honus lead the Pirates to a World Series championship?*

≫≫≫≫≫≫≫≫≫≫≫≫≫≫≫≫≫≫≫≫≫≫≫≫

Triple Crowns

WINNING A LEAGUE TITLE IN BATTING AVERAGE, HOME RUNS, AND RBI IS ONE OF THE RAREST FEATS IN BASEBALL.

Ted Williams of the Boston Red Sox is one of only two players to win a pair of Triple Crowns.

Jimmie Foxx

POSITION: First base **MLB CAREER: 1925–1945**

Jimmie Foxx followed in the footsteps of Babe Ruth as baseball's biggest slugger. In 1929, while helping Philadelphia win the first of two straight World Series, Jimmie began a record streak of 12 seasons with at least 30 homers and 100 RBI. He was also a good enough overall hitter to have 11 seasons with an average above .320. In 1933, he won the A.L. Triple Crown (leading a league in homers, RBI, and batting average). He moved from the Athletics to the Red Sox in 1936 and led the A.L. at least once in homers,

RBI, and average during his years in Boston. When he retired, his 534 homers were surpassed only by Babe Ruth. "Old Double X" was elected to the Hall of Fame in 1951.

BIRTH DATE: October 22, 1907
BORN IN: Sudlersville, MD
HEIGHT: 6'0" WEIGHT: 195
BATS: Right THROWS: Right

TRIVIA: *Who was Jimmie's Hall of Fame manager with the Philadelphia Athletics?*

>>

Lou Gehrig

POSITION: First base   **MLB CAREER: 1923–1939**

When you look at the numbers, Lou Gehrig's career was simply stunning. He had eight seasons of 140 or more RBI and nine seasons with more than 130 runs scored. Lou had 12 straight seasons of at least 25 homers and 100 RBI, with career highs of 49 homers (1934 and 1936) and 184 RBI (1930, the second-highest total ever). Lou won the Triple Crown in 1934 with 49 homers, 165 RBI, and a .363 average. Though famous as a slugger, his .340 career average is among the highest ever.

He also set a record (since broken by Cal Ripken, Jr.) by playing in 2,130 consecutive games. Sadly, Lou died in 1941 of a nerve disease that today bears his name.

BIRTH DATE: June 19, 1903
BORN IN: New York, NY
HEIGHT: 6'0"   **WEIGHT: 200**
BATS: Left   **THROWS: Left**

TRIVIA: *What was Lou's nickname, which was inspired by his consecutive games played streak?*

>>

Rogers Hornsby

POSITION: Second base   **MLB CAREER: 1915–1937**

Rogers Hornsby was arguably the greatest righthanded hitter of all time. His .358 career batting average trails only Ty Cobb's .366 on the all-time career list. From 1920 to 1925, "The Rajah" won six straight N.L. batting titles and *averaged* an amazing .397. His .424 average in 1924 was the second-highest single-season mark in the 20th century. Rogers wasn't just a high-average hitter. His all-around hitting skills helped him become one of only two players to win two Triple Crowns (1922 and 1925). He set an all-time record by leading the N.L. in slugging percentage 10 times. Rogers was elected to the Hall of Fame in 1942 and the All-Century Team in 1999.

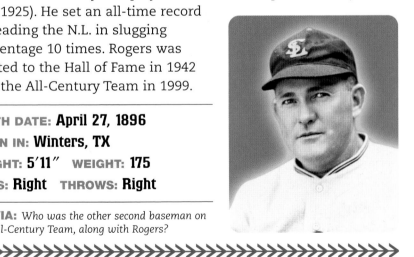

BIRTH DATE: April 27, 1896
BORN IN: Winters, TX
HEIGHT: 5′11″   WEIGHT: 175
BATS: Right   THROWS: Right

TRIVIA: *Who was the other second baseman on the All-Century Team, along with Rogers?*

Mickey Mantle

POSITION: **Outfield**   **MLB CAREER:** **1951–1968**

As great as Mickey Mantle was, many wondered how wonderful he would have been had he not been injured early in his career. "The Mick" combined incredible power with blazing speed as a young player, but knee and shoulder injuries slowed him over the years. His power never dimmed, however, and he hit numerous "tape-measure" home runs. One such blast traveled 565 feet during a 1953 game. The three-time A.L. MVP was also the best switch-hitter ever, generating power from both sides of

the plate. Also, no player had more career World Series homers or RBI. Mickey won the Triple Crown in 1956 and finished his career with 536 homers.

BIRTH DATE: **October 20, 1931**
BORN IN: **Spavinaw, OK**
HEIGHT: **5′11″**   **WEIGHT:** **198**
BATS: **Both**   **THROWS:** **Right**

TRIVIA: *What other great switch-hitter was elected to the Hall of Fame in 2002?*

>>

Frank Robinson

POSITION: Outfield, 1B   **MLB CAREER: 1956–1976**

Fifth all-time in career homers with 586, Frank Robinson was much more than a home run hitter. Frank is the only player ever to win MVP awards in both leagues (1961 with Cincinnati and 1966 with Baltimore). In 1966, he also won the Triple Crown (a career-high 49 homers along with 122 RBI and a .316 average) while helping the Orioles win the World Series. He helped Baltimore win it all again in 1970. Oh, yes, there were lots of homers along the way, too, including 11 seasons with more than 30 long balls. In 1975, Frank broke an important barrier, becoming the first African-American manager in the Majors, with Cleveland. He joined the Hall of Fame in 1982.

BIRTH DATE: August 31, 1935
BORN IN: Beaumont, TX
HEIGHT: 6'1"   **WEIGHT: 195**
BATS: Right   **THROWS: Right**

TRIVIA: *What did Frank do as the DH in his first at-bat as the player-manager of the Indians?*

>>

Ted Williams

POSITION: Outfield   **MLB CAREER: 1939–1960**

Many experts (including himself!) have considered Ted Williams to be the "greatest hitter who ever lived." Certainly no hitter ever worked harder to understand and perfect the craft. He won six A.L. batting titles, had a lifetime average of .344, and no batter since has topped his .406 average in 1941. Williams won two MVP awards and joins Rogers Hornsby as the only two-time Triple Crown winners (1942, 1947) in history. Williams was also a tremendous slugger, with 521 lifetime homers. His numbers would have been even better had he not twice left the game to serve as a fighter pilot in the Marines. "The Splendid Splinter" was named to the Hall of Fame in 1966.

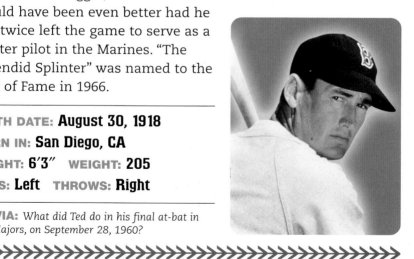

BIRTH DATE: August 30, 1918
BORN IN: San Diego, CA
HEIGHT: 6′3″   WEIGHT: 205
BATS: Left   THROWS: Right

TRIVIA: *What did Ted do in his final at-bat in the Majors, on September 28, 1960?*

>>

Carl Yastrzemski

POSITION: Outfield   **MLB CAREER: 1961–1983**

Steadiness and stardom were the hallmarks of Carl Yastrzemski's career. "Yaz" played with the Red Sox for a record 23 seasons and was named to 18 All-Star teams. On his way to a career total of 3,419 hits, he became the first A.L. player (and one of seven players ever) with 400 homers and 3,000 hits in a career, something that Babe Ruth, Lou Gehrig, and Ted Williams didn't accomplish. He is in the top 10 all-time in games, hits, at-bats, and doubles. He also won seven Gold Gloves. Yaz's 1967 season remains a classic. He became the last player to win the Triple Crown, leading the Red Sox to their "Impossible Dream" A.L. pennant. Yaz joined the Hall of Fame in 1989.

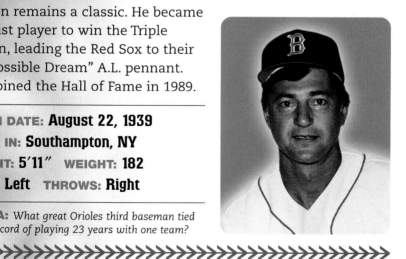

BIRTH DATE: August 22, 1939
BORN IN: Southampton, NY
HEIGHT: 5′11″   WEIGHT: 182
BATS: Left   THROWS: Right

TRIVIA: *What great Orioles third baseman tied Yaz's record of playing 23 years with one team?*

>>>>>>>>>>>>>>>>>>>>>>>>>>>>>>>>>>>>>>>

Statistics

THIS SECTION CONTAINS
COMPLETE CAREER
STATISTICS FOR ALL FIFTY
PLAYERS IN THIS BOOK
(UPDATED THROUGH 2003).

*Hall of Fame catcher Johnny
Bench had six seasons with 100
RBI for the Cincinnati Reds.*

Hank Aaron (for more information, see pages 32-33)

Year	Team	G	AB	R	H	2B	3B	HR	RBI	SB	AVG
1954	Mil. Braves	122	468	58	131	27	6	13	69	2	.280
1955	Mil. Braves	153	602	105	189	**37**	9	27	106	3	.314
1956	Mil. Braves	153	609	106	**200**	**34**	14	26	92	2	**.328**
1957	Mil. Braves	151	615	**118**	198	27	6	**44**	**132**	1	.322
1958	Mil. Braves	153	601	109	196	34	4	30	95	4	.326
1959	Mil. Braves	154	629	116	**223**	46	7	39	123	8	**.355**
1960	Mil. Braves	153	590	102	172	20	11	40	**126**	16	.292
1961	Mil. Braves	**155**	603	115	197	**39**	10	34	120	21	.327
1962	Mil. Braves	156	592	127	191	28	6	45	128	15	.323
1963	Mil. Braves	161	631	**121**	201	29	4	**44**	**130**	31	.319
1964	Mil. Braves	145	570	103	187	30	2	24	95	22	.328
1965	Mil. Braves	150	570	109	181	**40**	1	32	89	24	.318
1966	Atlanta	158	603	117	168	23	1	**44**	**127**	21	.279
1967	Atlanta	155	600	**113**	184	37	3	**39**	109	17	.307
1968	Atlanta	160	606	84	174	33	4	29	86	28	.287
1969	Atlanta	147	547	100	164	30	3	44	97	9	.300
1970	Atlanta	150	516	103	154	26	1	38	118	9	.298
1971	Atlanta	139	495	95	162	22	3	47	118	1	.327
1972	Atlanta	129	449	75	119	10	0	34	77	4	.265
1973	Atlanta	120	392	84	118	12	1	40	96	1	.301
1974	Atlanta	112	340	47	91	16	0	20	69	1	.268
1975	Mil. Brewers	137	465	45	109	16	2	12	60	0	.234
1976	Mil. Brewers	85	271	22	62	8	0	10	35	0	.229
Totals		3298	12364	2174	3771	624	98	755	2297	240	.305

Bold = Led league

Notes
> First-ballot Hall of Fame inductee (1982);
> Selected to 21 consecutive All-Star Game appearances (1955-1975);
> Played in three postseason series, including two World Series, hitting .364 with 3 home runs and 9 RBIs;
> National League Most Valuable Player (1957), and finished in the top ten 13 times;
> Won three Gold Glove outfield awards (1958-1960);
> Ranked in the all-time top three in six categories: home runs (first), RBI (first), at-bats (second), games (third), runs (third), and hits (third);
> Broke Babe Ruth's home run record on April 8, 1974, off L.A.'s Al Downing;
> Was a shortstop with Indianapolis in the Negro Leagues when signed by Braves.

Jeff Bagwell (for more information, see pages 62-63)

Year	Team	G	AB	R	H	2B	3B	HR	RBI	SB	AVG
1991	Houston	156	554	79	163	26	4	15	82	7	.294
1992	Houston	**162**	586	87	160	34	6	18	96	10	.273
1993	Houston	142	535	76	171	37	4	20	88	13	.320
1994	Houston	110	400	**104**	147	32	2	39	**116**	15	.368
1995	Houston	114	448	88	130	29	0	21	87	12	.290
1996	Houston	**162**	568	111	179	**48**	2	31	120	21	.315
1997	Houston	**162**	566	109	162	40	2	43	135	31	.286
1998	Houston	147	540	124	164	33	1	34	111	19	.304
1999	Houston	**162**	562	**143**	171	35	0	42	126	30	.304
2000	Houston	159	590	**152**	183	37	1	47	132	9	.310
2001	Houston	161	600	126	173	43	4	39	130	11	.288
2002	Houston	158	571	94	166	33	2	31	98	7	.291
2003	Houston	160	605	109	168	28	2	39	100	11	.278
Totals		1955	7125	1402	2137	455	30	419	1421	196	.300

Bold = Led league

Notes
>Four All-Star appearances (1994, 1996, 1997, 1999);
>National League Rookie of the Year (1991);
>National League Most Valuable Player (1994);
>National League Gold Glove winner at first base (1994);
>Only player in history with six consecutive seasons with at least 30 homers, 100 runs scored, 100 RBI, and 100 walks (1996–2001).
>Joined Jimmie Foxx, Lou Gehrig, and Babe Ruth as only players to ever have six consecutive seasons with 30 homers, 100 RBI, and 100 runs scored;
>Just the fifth player to reach 300 homers, 1,000 RBI, 1,000 runs scored, and 1,000 walks in his first 11 seasons (joining Mickey Mantle, Eddie Mathews, Frank Thomas, and Ted Williams);
>His 152 runs scored in 2000 were the most by a National Leaguer since 1932;
>Only the fifth player to post a 45-homer, 100-RBI, 150 run scored season (along with Joe DiMaggio, Jimmie Foxx, Lou Gehrig, and Babe Ruth);
>Joins Barry Bonds as the only players to have more than one 40-homer, 30-steal season (1997 and 1999);
>Involved in possibly the most lopsided one-for-one trade in history, as Bagwell was traded by the Boston Red Sox to the Astros for pitcher Larry Andersen (August 30, 1990), and Andersen pitched just 22 innings for the Red Sox.

Ernie Banks (for more information, see pages 34-35)

Year	Team	G	AB	R	H	2B	3B	HR	RBI	SB	AVG
1953	Chicago Cubs	10	35	3	11	1	1	2	6	0	.314
1954	Chicago Cubs	**154**	593	70	163	19	7	19	79	6	.275
1955	Chicago Cubs	**154**	596	98	176	29	9	44	117	9	.295
1956	Chicago Cubs	139	538	82	160	25	8	28	85	6	.297
1957	Chicago Cubs	**156**	594	113	169	34	6	43	102	8	.285
1958	Chicago Cubs	**154**	**617**	119	193	23	11	**47**	**129**	4	.313
1959	Chicago Cubs	**155**	589	97	179	25	6	45	**143**	2	.304
1960	Chicago Cubs	**156**	597	94	162	32	7	**41**	117	1	.271
1961	Chicago Cubs	138	511	75	142	22	4	29	80	1	.278
1962	Chicago Cubs	154	610	87	164	20	6	37	104	5	.269
1963	Chicago Cubs	130	432	41	98	20	1	18	64	0	.227
1964	Chicago Cubs	157	591	67	156	29	6	23	95	1	.264
1965	Chicago Cubs	163	612	79	162	25	3	28	106	3	.265
1966	Chicago Cubs	141	511	52	139	23	7	15	75	0	.272
1967	Chicago Cubs	151	573	68	158	26	4	23	95	2	.276
1968	Chicago Cubs	150	552	71	136	27	0	32	83	2	.246
1969	Chicago Cubs	155	565	60	143	19	2	23	106	0	.253
1970	Chicago Cubs	72	222	25	56	6	2	12	44	0	.252
1971	Chicago Cubs	39	83	4	16	2	0	3	6	0	.193
Totals		2528	9421	1305	2583	407	90	512	1636	50	.274

Bold = Led league

Notes
>First-ballot Hall of Fame inductee (1977);
>Eleven-time All Star (1955–1962, 1965, 1967, 1969);
>Two-time National League MVP (1958, 1959);
>Won National League Gold Glove at shortstop (1960);
>From 1955–1960 hit more home runs (248) than any player in the majors, including Hank Aaron, Mickey Mantle, and Willie Mays;
>His 44 homers in 1955 were, at that time, a single-season record for a shortstop;
>Played in the Negro Leagues, and spent two years in the Army, before the Cubs signed him at the age of 22;
>The first Cubs player to have his uniform number (14) retired;
>Remembered as one of baseball's best hitting shortstops, Banks actually played more games at first base (1,259) than shortstop (1,125).

Johnny Bench (for more information, see pages 64-65)

Year	Team	G	AB	R	H	2B	3B	HR	RBI	SB	AVG
1967	Cincinnati	26	86	7	14	3	1	1	6	0	.163
1968	Cincinnati	154	564	67	155	40	2	15	82	1	.275
1969	Cincinnati	148	532	83	156	23	1	26	90	6	.293
1970	Cincinnati	158	605	97	177	35	4	**45**	**148**	5	.293
1971	Cincinnati	149	562	80	134	19	2	27	61	2	.238
1972	Cincinnati	147	538	87	145	22	2	**40**	**125**	6	.270
1973	Cincinnati	152	557	83	141	17	3	25	104	4	.253
1974	Cincinnati	160	621	108	174	38	2	33	**129**	5	.280
1975	Cincinnati	142	530	83	150	39	1	28	110	11	.283
1976	Cincinnati	135	465	62	109	24	1	16	74	13	.234
1977	Cincinnati	142	494	67	136	34	2	31	109	2	.275
1978	Cincinnati	120	393	52	102	17	1	23	73	4	.260
1979	Cincinnati	130	464	73	128	19	0	22	80	4	.276
1980	Cincinnati	114	360	52	90	12	0	24	68	4	.250
1981	Cincinnati	52	178	14	55	8	0	8	25	0	.309
1982	Cincinnati	119	399	44	103	16	0	13	38	1	.258
1983	Cincinnati	110	310	32	79	15	2	12	54	0	.255
Totals		2158	7658	1091	2048	381	24	389	1376	68	.267

Bold = Led league

Notes
>First-ballot Hall of Fame inductee (1989);
>Fourteen-time All Star (1968-1980, 1983);
>Played in 10 postseason series, including hitting .279 with 5 home runs and 14 RBI in four World Series, and was 1976 World Series MVP with a .533 average and 2 homers and 6 RBI in 4 games;
>Two-time National League MVP (1970, 1972);
>Was first catcher to win National League Rookie of the Year (1968);
>Won 10 consecutive Gold Gloves at catcher (1968–1977);
>At the time of his retirement, owned single-season (38 in 1970) and career (327) records for home runs hit while playing catcher;
>In his final three seasons, split most of his defensive duties between third base and first base.
>At spring training in 1968, prior to Bench's first full season, Ted Williams autographed a ball, "To Johnny Bench, a Hall of Famer for sure."

Yogi Berra (for more information, see pages 66-67)

Year	Team	G	AB	R	H	2B	3B	HR	RBI	SB	AVG
1946	N.Y. Yankees	7	22	3	8	1	0	2	4	0	.364
1947	N.Y. Yankees	83	293	41	82	15	3	11	54	0	.280
1948	N.Y. Yankees	125	469	70	143	24	10	14	98	3	.305
1949	N.Y. Yankees	116	415	59	115	20	2	20	91	2	.277
1950	N.Y. Yankees	151	597	116	192	30	6	28	124	4	.322
1951	N.Y. Yankees	141	547	92	161	19	4	27	88	5	.294
1952	N.Y. Yankees	142	534	97	146	17	1	30	98	2	.273
1953	N.Y. Yankees	137	503	80	149	23	5	27	108	0	.296
1954	N.Y. Yankees	151	584	88	179	28	6	22	125	0	.307
1955	N.Y. Yankees	147	541	84	147	20	3	27	108	1	.272
1956	N.Y. Yankees	140	521	93	155	29	2	30	105	3	.298
1957	N.Y. Yankees	134	482	74	121	14	2	24	82	1	.251
1958	N.Y. Yankees	122	433	60	115	17	3	22	90	3	.266
1959	N.Y. Yankees	131	472	64	134	25	1	19	69	1	.284
1960	N.Y. Yankees	120	359	46	99	14	1	15	62	2	.276
1961	N.Y. Yankees	119	395	62	107	11	0	22	61	2	.271
1962	N.Y. Yankees	86	232	25	52	8	0	10	35	0	.224
1963	N.Y. Yankees	64	147	20	43	6	0	8	28	1	.293
1965	N.Y. Mets	4	9	1	2	0	0	0	0	0	.222
Totals		2120	7555	1175	2150	321	49	358	1430	30	.285

Notes
>Hall of Fame inductee (1972);
>Selected to 15 consecutive All-Star appearances (1948-1962);
>Played in 14 World Series, hitting .274 with 12 home runs and 39 RBIs, and holds World Series record for games (75), at-bats (259), and hits (71);
>Three-time American League MVP (1951, 1954, 1955), and ranked in the top four in MVP voting seven consecutive seasons (1950-56);
>Despite the fact he was a notorious bad-ball hitter, Berra never struck out more than 38 times in a season;
>Managed five full seasons, twice guiding his team to the World Series (1964 Yankees, 1973 Mets) only to lose in seven games both times.

Wade Boggs (for more information, see pages 8-9)

Year	Team	G	AB	R	H	2B	3B	HR	RBI	SB	AVG
1982	Boston	104	338	51	118	14	1	5	44	1	.349
1983	Boston	153	582	100	210	44	7	5	74	3	**.361**
1984	Boston	158	625	109	203	31	4	6	55	3	.325
1985	Boston	161	653	107	**240**	42	3	8	78	2	**.368**
1986	Boston	149	580	107	207	47	2	8	71	0	**.357**
1987	Boston	147	551	108	200	40	6	24	89	1	**.363**
1988	Boston	155	584	**128**	214	**45**	6	5	58	2	**.366**
1989	Boston	156	621	**113**	205	**51**	7	3	54	2	.330
1990	Boston	155	619	89	187	44	5	6	63	0	.302
1991	Boston	144	546	93	181	42	2	8	51	1	.332
1992	Boston	143	514	62	133	22	4	7	50	1	.259
1993	N.Y. Yankees	143	560	83	169	26	1	2	59	0	.302
1994	N.Y. Yankees	97	366	61	125	19	1	11	55	2	.342
1995	N.Y. Yankees	126	460	76	149	22	4	5	63	1	.324
1996	N.Y. Yankees	132	501	80	156	29	2	2	41	1	.311
1997	N.Y. Yankees	104	353	55	103	23	1	4	28	0	.292
1998	Tampa Bay	123	435	51	122	23	4	7	52	3	.280
1999	Tampa Bay	90	292	40	88	14	1	2	29	1	.301
Totals		2439	9180	1513	3010	578	61	118	1014	24	.328

Bold = Led league

Notes

> Twelve-time All Star (1985–1996);
> Played in nine postseason series, including hitting .286 in 42 at-bats in two World Series (1986, 1996);
> Two-time American League Gold Glove winner at third base (1994, 1995);
> Finished in the top five in batting average 11 times during his career;
> Led the American League in on-base percentage six times;
> Had at least 200 hits in seven consecutive seasons, the longest such streak by any player who did not play in the 1800s;
> Despite being one of the least powerful hitters of the 25 players in the 3,000-hit club, Boggs' 3,000th hit was, ironically, a home run, on August 7, 1999 against Chris Haney of the Cleveland Indians;
> Was extremely superstitious: he ate chicken before every game, stepped into the batting cage at 5:17, and began running wind sprints at 7:17 prior to 7:30 games

Barry Bonds (for more information, see pages 36-37)

Year	Team	G	AB	R	H	2B	3B	HR	RBI	SB	AVG
1986	Pittsburgh	113	413	72	92	26	3	16	48	36	.223
1987	Pittsburgh	150	551	99	144	34	9	25	59	32	.261
1988	Pittsburgh	144	538	97	152	30	5	24	58	17	.283
1989	Pittsburgh	159	580	96	144	34	6	19	58	32	.248
1990	Pittsburgh	151	519	104	156	32	3	33	114	52	.301
1991	Pittsburgh	153	510	95	149	28	5	25	116	43	.292
1992	Pittsburgh	140	473	**109**	147	36	5	34	103	39	.311
1993	San Francisco	159	539	129	181	38	4	**46**	**123**	29	.336
1994	San Francisco	112	391	89	122	18	1	37	81	29	.312
1995	San Francisco	**144**	506	109	149	30	7	33	104	31	.294
1996	San Francisco	158	517	122	159	27	3	42	129	40	.308
1997	San Francisco	159	532	123	155	26	5	40	101	37	.291
1998	San Francisco	156	552	120	167	44	7	37	122	28	.303
1999	San Francisco	102	355	91	93	20	2	34	83	15	.262
2000	San Francisco	143	480	129	147	28	4	49	106	11	.306
2001	San Francisco	153	476	129	156	32	2	**73**	137	13	.328
2002	San Francisco	143	403	117	149	31	2	46	110	9	**.370**
2003	San Francisco	130	390	111	133	22	1	45	90	7	.341
Totals		2569	8725	1941	2595	536	74	658	1742	500	.297

Bold = Led league

Notes
>Selected to 12 All-Star appearances (1990, 1992–98, 2000–03);
>In 2002, set records for a single postseason with 8 homers (in just 45 at-bats) and walks (27);
>Won record six National League MVP awards (1990, 1992, 1993, 2001–2003), and finished in the top ten 12 times;
>Won eight National League outfield Gold Glove awards (1990–94, 1996–98);
>Owns record for home runs in a season (73 in 2001), breaking Mark McGwire's record of 70 set in 1998;
>Only player in history with 500 home runs and 500 stolen bases;
>Shares record of five 30-homer, 30-steal seasons with father Bobby Bonds;
>Joins Jose Canseco and Alex Rodriguez as only players to post a 40-40 season;
>Set single-season records for on-base percentage (.582) and walks (198) in 2002;
>Ranks in the top ten in: homers, on-base percentage, runs, slugging percentage;
>Joins Jimmie Foxx as only players with 12 consecutive 30-homer seasons.

Lou Brock (for more information, see pages 86-87)

Year	Team	G	AB	R	H	2B	3B	HR	RBI	SB	AVG
1961	Chicago Cubs	4	11	1	1	0	0	0	0	0	.091
1962	Chicago Cubs	123	434	73	114	24	7	9	35	16	.263
1963	Chicago Cubs	148	547	79	141	19	11	9	37	24	.258
1964	Chicago Cubs	52	215	30	54	9	2	2	14	10	.251
1964	St. Louis	103	419	81	146	21	9	12	44	33	.348
1965	St. Louis	155	631	107	182	35	8	16	69	63	.288
1966	St. Louis	156	643	94	183	24	12	15	46	**74**	.285
1967	St. Louis	159	**689**	**113**	206	32	12	21	76	**52**	.299
1968	St. Louis	159	660	92	184	**46**	**14**	6	51	**62**	.279
1969	St. Louis	157	655	97	195	33	10	12	47	**53**	.298
1970	St. Louis	155	664	114	202	29	5	13	57	51	.304
1971	St. Louis	157	640	**126**	200	37	7	7	61	**64**	.313
1972	St. Louis	153	621	81	193	26	8	3	42	**63**	.311
1973	St. Louis	160	650	110	193	29	8	7	63	**70**	.297
1974	St. Louis	153	635	105	194	25	7	3	48	**118**	.306
1975	St. Louis	136	528	78	163	27	6	3	47	56	.309
1976	St. Louis	133	498	73	150	24	5	4	67	56	.301
1977	St. Louis	141	489	69	133	22	6	2	46	35	.272
1978	St. Louis	92	298	31	66	9	0	0	12	17	.221
1979	St. Louis	120	405	56	123	15	4	5	38	21	.304
Totals		2616	10332	1610	3023	486	141	149	900	938	.293

Bold = Led league

Notes
>First-ballot Hall of Fame inductee (1985);
>Six All-Star appearances (1967, 1971, 1972, 1974, 1975, 1979);
>Played in three World Series, hitting .391 in 87 at-bats with 4 home runs, 13 RBI, and a record-tying 14 stolen bases, including twice setting the record for most steals in a single World Series when he stole 7 bases in both 1967 and 1968;
>First player to hit 20 home runs and steal 50 bases in a season (1967);
>Broke Ty Cobb's record for career stolen bases, and held mark for 14 years until surpassed by Rickey Henderson;
>Set National League record for stolen bases in a season (118 in 1974);
>Only player to steal at least 50 bases in 12 consecutive seasons;
>In arguably the worst trade in Cubs history, was in a six-man trade in 1964 that was essentially Brock for pitcher Ernie Broglio, who went 7-19 before retiring.

Rod Carew (for more information, see pages 10-11)

Year	Team	G	AB	R	H	2B	3B	HR	RBI	SB	AVG
1967	Minnesota	137	514	66	150	22	7	8	51	5	.292
1968	Minnesota	127	461	46	126	27	2	1	42	12	.273
1969	Minnesota	123	458	79	152	30	4	8	56	19	**.332**
1970	Minnesota	51	191	27	70	12	3	4	28	4	.366
1971	Minnesota	147	577	88	177	16	10	2	48	6	.307
1972	Minnesota	142	535	61	170	21	6	0	51	12	**.318**
1973	Minnesota	149	580	98	**203**	30	**11**	6	62	41	**.350**
1974	Minnesota	153	599	86	**218**	30	5	3	55	38	**.364**
1975	Minnesota	143	535	89	192	24	4	14	80	35	**.359**
1976	Minnesota	156	605	97	200	29	12	9	90	49	.331
1977	Minnesota	155	616	**128**	**239**	38	**16**	14	100	23	**.388**
1978	Minnesota	152	564	85	188	26	10	5	70	27	**.333**
1979	California	110	409	78	130	15	3	3	44	18	.318
1980	California	144	540	74	179	34	7	3	59	23	.331
1981	California	93	364	57	111	17	1	2	21	16	.305
1982	California	138	523	88	167	25	5	3	44	10	.319
1983	California	129	472	66	160	24	2	2	44	6	.339
1984	California	93	329	42	97	8	1	3	31	4	.295
1985	California	127	443	69	124	17	3	2	39	5	.280
Totals		2469	9315	1424	3053	445	112	92	1015	353	.328

Bold = Led league

Notes
>First-ballot Hall of Fame inductee (1991);
>Selected to 18 consecutive All-Star appearances (1967–1984), the first nine years as a second baseman and the second nine as a first baseman;
>American League Rookie of the Year (1967) and American League MVP (1977);
>One of just five players (Ty Cobb, Stan Musial, Honus Wagner, and Tony Gwynn) to hit at least .300 for 15 consecutive seasons;
>Became first (and only) player to win a batting title without a home run (1972);
>Won six batting titles in seven years, and the year he lost (1976), he hit .331 to finish behind George Brett (.333) and Hal McRae (.332);
>Stole home 7 times in 1969, one short of Ty Cobb's single-season record;
>Is second among players since 1945 with 17 steals of home (Jackie Robinson).

Roberto Clemente (for more information, see pages 12-13)

Year	Team	G	AB	R	H	2B	3B	HR	RBI	SB	AVG
1955	Pittsburgh	124	474	48	121	23	11	5	47	2	.255
1956	Pittsburgh	147	543	66	169	30	7	7	60	6	.311
1957	Pittsburgh	111	451	42	114	17	7	4	30	0	.253
1958	Pittsburgh	140	519	69	150	24	10	6	50	8	.289
1959	Pittsburgh	105	432	60	128	17	7	4	50	2	.296
1960	Pittsburgh	144	570	89	179	22	6	16	94	4	.314
1961	Pittsburgh	146	572	100	201	30	10	23	89	4	**.351**
1962	Pittsburgh	144	538	95	168	28	9	10	74	6	.312
1963	Pittsburgh	152	600	77	192	23	8	17	76	12	.320
1964	Pittsburgh	155	622	95	**211**	40	7	12	87	5	**.339**
1965	Pittsburgh	152	589	91	194	21	14	10	65	8	**.329**
1966	Pittsburgh	154	638	105	202	31	11	29	119	7	.317
1967	Pittsburgh	147	585	103	**209**	26	10	23	110	9	**.357**
1968	Pittsburgh	132	502	74	146	18	12	18	57	2	.291
1969	Pittsburgh	138	507	87	175	20	**12**	19	91	4	.345
1970	Pittsburgh	108	412	65	145	22	10	14	60	3	.352
1971	Pittsburgh	132	522	82	178	29	8	13	86	1	.341
1972	Pittsburgh	102	378	68	118	19	7	10	60	0	.312
Totals		2433	9454	1416	3000	440	166	240	1305	83	.317

Bold = Led league

Notes

>Five-year waiting period was waived, making him a first-ballot Hall of Fame inductee (1973), becoming the first Latin American-born player enshrined in Cooperstown;

>Twelve-time All Star (1960–1967, 1969–1972);

>Played in five postseason series, including hitting .362 in 58 at-bats in two World Series (1960, 1971), hit safely in all 14 games, and was the 1971 MVP;

>Led the National League in assists five times, a record for an outfielder;

>Won twelve consecutive National League outfield Gold Glove awards (1961–1972);

>Has the second-most triples by a player who played after 1945 (trailing Stan Musial);

>Recorded his 3,000th hit in his final at-bat of the 1972 season;

>Was signed by the Dodgers in 1954, but the Dodgers did not protect him on their 40-man roster after the season and Pittsburgh general manager Branch Rickey, once the Dodgers' general manager, drafted Clemente for $4,000.

Ty Cobb (for more information, see pages 88-89)

Year	Team	G	AB	R	H	2B	3B	HR	RBI	SB	AVG
1905	Detroit	41	150	19	36	6	0	1	15	2	.240
1906	Detroit	98	350	45	112	13	7	1	34	23	.320
1907	Detroit	150	605	97	212	28	14	5	119	49	.350
1908	Detroit	150	581	88	188	36	20	4	108	39	.324
1909	Detroit	156	573	116	216	33	10	9	107	76	.377
1910	Detroit	140	509	106	196	36	13	8	91	65	.385
1911	Detroit	146	591	147	248	47	24	8	127	83	.420
1912	Detroit	140	553	119	227	30	23	7	83	61	.410
1913	Detroit	122	428	70	167	18	16	4	67	51	.390
1914	Detroit	98	345	69	127	22	11	2	57	35	.368
1915	Detroit	156	563	144	208	31	13	3	99	96	.369
1916	Detroit	145	542	113	201	31	10	5	68	68	.371
1917	Detroit	152	588	107	225	44	24	6	102	55	.383
1918	Detroit	111	421	83	161	19	14	3	64	34	.382
1919	Detroit	124	497	92	191	36	13	1	70	28	.384
1920	Detroit	112	428	86	143	28	8	2	63	15	.334
1921	Detroit	128	507	124	197	37	16	12	101	22	.389
1922	Detroit	137	526	99	211	42	16	4	99	9	.401
1923	Detroit	145	556	103	189	40	7	6	88	9	.340
1924	Detroit	155	625	115	211	38	10	4	79	23	.338
1925	Detroit	121	415	97	157	31	12	12	102	13	.378
1926	Detroit	79	233	48	79	18	5	4	62	9	.339
1927	Phil. Athletics	134	490	104	175	32	7	5	93	22	.357
1928	Phil. Athletics	95	353	54	114	27	4	1	40	5	.323
Totals		**3035**	**11434**	**2246**	**4189**	**724**	**295**	**117**	**1937**	**892**	**.366**

Bold = Led league

Notes
>One of five charter members elected into Hall of Fame (1936);
>Played in three World Series (1907–1909), hitting .262 with 9 RBI and 4 steals;
>American League Triple Crown winner (1909);
>Set records for best career batting average (.366), most consecutive years leading league in average (9), most times leading league in average (12), most years hitting over .300 (23), and most consecutive years hitting over .300 (23);
>No. 1 all-time in batting average; also ranks in the top six in: hits (second), runs (second), triples (second), doubles (fourth), stolen bases (fourth), games (fifth), at-bats (fifth), and RBI (sixth).

Carlos Delgado (for more information, see pages 68-69)

Year	Team	G	AB	R	H	2B	3B	HR	RBI	SB	AVG
1993	Toronto	2	1	0	0	0	0	0	0	0	.000
1994	Toronto	43	130	17	28	2	0	9	24	1	.215
1995	Toronto	37	91	7	15	3	0	3	11	0	.165
1996	Toronto	138	488	68	132	28	2	25	92	0	.270
1997	Toronto	153	519	79	136	42	3	30	91	0	.262
1998	Toronto	142	530	94	155	43	1	38	115	3	.292
1999	Toronto	152	573	113	156	39	0	44	134	1	.272
2000	Toronto	**162**	569	115	196	**57**	1	41	137	0	.344
2001	Toronto	**162**	574	102	160	31	1	39	102	3	.279
2002	Toronto	143	505	103	140	34	2	33	108	1	.277
2003	Toronto	161	570	117	172	38	1	42	**145**	0	.302
Totals		1295	4550	815	1290	317	11	304	959	9	.284

Bold = Led league

Notes

>Appeared in two All-Star Games (2000, 2003);

>Became fifteenth player in Major League history to hit 4 home runs in a game (September 25, 2003), and just the sixth player to hit all 4 homers in consecutive at-bats;

>Finished fourth in the American League Most Valuable Player voting in 2000, when he led league in doubles, extra-base hits, and total bases, was second in walks, on-base percentage, and slugging percentage, fourth in average, and tied for fourth in home runs and RBI;

>One of just four players to have posted 30 homers and 100 RBI each of the past six seasons, 1998–2003 (Rafael Palmeiro, Jim Thome, and Alex Rodriguez);

>Holds Blue Jays club record for career home runs;

>In 2003, led the majors in RBI and led the American League in OPS (on-base plus slugging percentage) at 1.019;

>Shares record for most homers by a rookie in the month of April (8 in 1994, joining Kent Hrbek);

>Played catcher in the minors before switching to first base.

Joe DiMaggio (for more information, see pages 14-15)

Year	Team	G	AB	R	H	2B	3B	HR	RBI	SB	AVG
1936	N.Y. Yankees	138	637	132	206	44	**15**	29	125	4	.323
1937	N.Y. Yankees	151	621	**151**	215	35	15	**46**	167	3	.346
1938	N.Y. Yankees	145	599	129	194	32	13	32	140	6	.324
1939	N.Y. Yankees	120	462	108	176	32	6	30	126	3	**.381**
1940	N.Y. Yankees	132	508	93	179	28	9	31	133	1	**.352**
1941	N.Y. Yankees	139	541	122	193	43	11	30	**125**	4	.357
1942	N.Y. Yankees	154	610	123	186	29	13	21	114	4	.305
1946	N.Y. Yankees	132	503	81	146	20	8	25	95	1	.290
1947	N.Y. Yankees	141	534	97	168	31	10	20	97	3	.315
1948	N.Y. Yankees	153	594	110	190	26	11	**39**	**155**	1	.320
1949	N.Y. Yankees	76	272	58	94	14	6	14	67	0	.346
1950	N.Y. Yankees	139	525	114	158	33	10	32	122	0	.301
1951	N.Y. Yankees	116	415	72	109	22	4	12	71	0	.263
Totals		1736	6821	1390	2214	389	131	361	1537	30	.325

Bold = Led league

Notes

>Inducted into Hall of Fame (1955);

>Selected to All-Star Game all 13 seasons of his career;

>Played in 10 World Series (1936–1939, 1941–1942, 1947, 1949–1951), posting a .271 average with 8 home runs and 30 RBI in 199 at-bats;

>Three-time American League MVP (1939, 1941, 1947), and finished in the top 10 in MVP voting 10 times;

>Set a Major League record with a 56-game hitting streak in 1941—the next longest streak is 44 games (Willie Keeler and Pete Rose). Eight years earlier, as an 18-year-old minor leaguer, DiMaggio had a 61-game hitting streak;

>Hit 361 home runs and struck out just 369 times in his career, by far the best homer-to-strikeout ratio of anyone with more than 300 lifetime home runs;

>Was injured with a sore heel for the first two months of 1949, but returned to help the Yankees to another World Series title;

>Missed three seasons (1943–1945) while serving in World War II;

>Was briefly married to actress Marilyn Monroe after his playing career.

Jimmie Foxx (for more information, see pages 102-103)

Year	Team	G	AB	R	H	2B	3B	HR	RBI	SB	AVG
1925	Phil. Athletics	10	9	2	6	1	0	0	0	0	.667
1926	Phil. Athletics	26	32	8	10	2	1	0	5	1	.313
1927	Phil. Athletics	61	130	23	42	6	5	3	20	2	.323
1928	Phil. Athletics	118	400	85	131	29	10	13	79	3	.328
1929	Phil. Athletics	149	517	123	183	23	9	33	118	9	.354
1930	Phil. Athletics	153	562	127	188	33	13	37	156	7	.335
1931	Phil. Athletics	139	515	93	150	32	10	30	120	4	.291
1932	Phil. Athletics	154	585	**151**	213	33	9	**58**	**169**	3	.364
1933	Phil. Athletics	149	573	125	204	37	9	**48**	163	2	**.356**
1934	Phil. Athletics	150	539	120	180	28	6	44	130	11	.334
1935	Phil. Athletics	147	535	118	185	33	7	**36**	115	6	.346
1936	Boston	**155**	585	130	198	32	8	41	143	13	.338
1937	Boston	150	569	111	162	24	6	36	127	10	.285
1938	Boston	149	565	139	197	33	9	50	**175**	5	**.349**
1939	Boston	124	467	130	168	31	10	**35**	105	4	.360
1940	Boston	144	515	106	153	30	4	36	119	4	.297
1941	Boston	135	487	87	146	27	8	19	105	2	.300
1942	Boston	30	100	18	27	4	0	5	14	0	.270
1942	Chicago Cubs	70	205	25	42	8	0	3	19	1	.205
1944	Chicago Cubs	15	20	0	1	1	0	0	2	0	.050
1945	Phil. Phillies	89	224	30	60	11	1	7	38	0	.268
Totals		2317	8134	1751	2646	458	125	534	1922	87	.325

Bold = Led league

Notes

>Inducted into Hall of Fame (1951);
>Played in each of the first nine All-Star Games (1933–1941);
>Participated in three World Series (1929–1931), hitting .344 with 4 home runs in 64 career at-bats;
>Three-time American League MVP (1932, 1933, 1938);
>Won American League Triple Crown (1933);
>Seventh all-time in RBI, and shares record with 13 consecutive 100-RBI seasons;
>Played with Ty Cobb (1927–1928) and Ted Williams (1939–1942);
>Originally entered the majors as a catcher, and in addition to first base, he played more than 100 career games at third base (141) and catcher (108).

Nomar Garciaparra (for more information, see pages 70-71)

Year	Team	G	AB	R	H	2B	3B	HR	RBI	SB	AVG
1996	Boston	24	87	11	21	2	3	4	16	5	.241
1997	Boston	153	**684**	122	**209**	44	**11**	30	98	22	.306
1998	Boston	143	604	111	195	37	8	35	122	12	.323
1999	Boston	135	532	103	190	42	4	27	104	14	**.357**
2000	Boston	140	529	104	197	51	3	21	96	5	**.372**
2001	Boston	21	83	13	24	3	0	4	8	0	.289
2002	Boston	156	635	101	197	**56**	5	24	120	5	.310
2003	Boston	156	658	120	198	37	13	28	105	19	.301
Totals		**928**	**3812**	**685**	**1231**	**272**	**47**	**173**	**669**	**82**	**.323**

Bold = Led league

Notes
>Selected to five All-Star Games (1997, 1999, 2000, 2002, 2003);
>Played in three postseason series, hitting .323 with 7 home runs and 21 RBI;
>American League Rookie of the Year Award (1997);
>Is the first right-handed American League hitter to win consecutive batting titles since Joe DiMaggio (1939–1940);
>Set single-season record for doubles by a shortstop (56 in 2002);
>One of six players to hit at least 30 homers in each of his first two full seasons;
>Established American League rookie record with a 30-game hitting streak (1997);
>Owns record for most home runs by a rookie shortstop (30), breaking the record of 22 previously set by Ron Hansen (1960);
>Reached 1,000 career hits in fewer games (746) than anyone in Red Sox history;
>Hit 2 grand slams in a game against Seattle (May 10, 1999), marking the eleventh time in Major League history that has taken place;
>In 2003, finished second in the American League in runs (120) and triples (13);
>Originally drafted out of high school by the Milwaukee Brewers in 1991, but opted to attend Georgia Tech University, and was then drafted by the Red Sox in 1994.

Lou Gehrig (for more information, see pages 104-105)

Year	Team	G	AB	R	H	2B	3B	HR	RBI	SB	AVG
1923	N.Y. Yankees	13	26	6	11	4	1	1	9	0	.423
1924	N.Y. Yankees	10	12	2	6	1	0	0	5	0	.500
1925	N.Y. Yankees	126	437	73	129	23	10	20	68	6	.295
1926	N.Y. Yankees	155	572	135	179	47	**20**	16	112	6	.313
1927	N.Y. Yankees	**155**	584	149	218	**52**	18	47	**175**	10	.373
1928	N.Y. Yankees	154	562	139	210	**47**	13	27	**142**	4	.374
1929	N.Y. Yankees	154	553	127	166	32	10	35	126	4	.300
1930	N.Y. Yankees	**154**	581	143	220	42	17	41	**174**	12	.379
1931	N.Y. Yankees	155	619	**163**	**211**	31	15	**46**	**184**	17	.341
1932	N.Y. Yankees	**156**	596	138	208	42	9	34	151	4	.349
1933	N.Y. Yankees	152	593	**138**	198	41	12	32	139	9	.334
1934	N.Y. Yankees	**154**	579	128	210	40	6	**49**	165	9	**.363**
1935	N.Y. Yankees	149	535	**125**	176	26	10	30	119	8	.329
1936	N.Y. Yankees	**155**	579	**167**	205	37	7	**49**	152	3	.354
1937	N.Y. Yankees	**157**	569	138	200	37	9	37	159	4	.351
1938	N.Y. Yankees	**157**	576	115	170	32	6	29	114	6	.295
1939	N.Y. Yankees	8	28	2	4	0	0	0	1	0	.143
Totals		2164	8001	1888	2721	534	163	493	1995	102	.340

Bold = Led league

Notes

> Five-year waiting period was waived, and Gehrig was elected to the Hall of Fame within a few months of his retirement (1939);
> Selected to the first seven All-Star Games (1933–1939);
> Played in seven World Series, hitting .361 in 119 at-bats with 10 home runs and 35 RBI, including a record-setting 4 homers in a 4-game series (1928);
> American League Most Valuable Player (1927, 1936);
> Won American League Triple Crown (1934);
> Ranks in the top 10 in numerous categories, including: on-base percentage (.447, fifth), RBI (fourth), slugging percentage (.632, third), and runs (tenth);
> Earned the nickname "The Iron Horse" as he established the record for consecutive games played (2,130) until surpassed by Cal Ripken in 1995;
> Hit Major League record 23 grand slams;
> Established American League record for RBI in a season (184 in 1931);
> Forced to retire because of a muscular disease (amyotrophic lateral sclerosis), known ever since as Lou Gehrig's disease, and passed away at age 37 in 1941.

Jason Giambi (for more information, see pages 72-73)

Year	Team	G	AB	R	H	2B	3B	HR	RBI	SB	AVG
1995	Oakland	54	176	27	45	7	0	6	25	2	.256
1996	Oakland	140	536	84	156	40	1	20	79	0	.291
1997	Oakland	142	519	66	152	41	2	20	81	0	.293
1998	Oakland	153	562	92	166	28	0	27	110	2	.295
1999	Oakland	158	575	115	181	36	1	33	123	1	.315
2000	Oakland	152	510	108	170	29	1	43	137	2	.333
2001	Oakland	154	520	109	178	**47**	2	38	120	2	.342
2002	N.Y. Yankees	155	560	120	176	34	1	41	122	2	.314
2003	N.Y. Yankees	156	535	97	134	25	0	41	107	2	.250
Totals		1264	4493	818	1358	287	8	269	904	13	.302

Bold = Led league

Notes

>Appeared in four All-Star Games (2000–2003);
>Played in six postseason series, including the 2003 World Series in which he hit .235 with 1 home run in 17 at-bats.
>American League Most Valuable Player award winner (2000);
>First Yankees player to post consecutive 40-homer seasons since Mickey Mantle (1960–1961);
>Ranked first or second in the American League in walks for five consecutive seasons (1999–2003);
>Has been on base more than any player in the majors the past five seasons (1,513 compared to Barry Bonds having reached base 1,425 times);
>Led American League in on-base percentage twice (2000 and 2001), and ranked third in the league two other times (2002 and 2003);
>Ranked in the top seven in the American League in home runs four consecutive seasons (2000–2003), and in the top eight in RBI each of the last five seasons (1999–2003);
>In 2002, along with brother, Jeremy, set Major League record for most home runs by brothers in a season with 61, when Jason hit 41 and Jeremy hit 20 for Oakland and Philadelphia (breaking the mark of 59 set by Joe, 46, and Vince, 13, DiMaggio in 1937 and Joe, 30, Vince, 21, and Dom, 8, DiMaggio in 1941).

Josh Gibson (for more information, see pages 38-39)

Year	Team	G	AB	R	H	2B	3B	HR	RBI	SB	AVG
1930	Homestead Grays	10	33		8	1	0	1		1	.242
1931	Homestead Grays	32	128		47	8	4	**6**		0	.367
1932	Homestead Grays	**46**	147		42	3	**5**	**7**		1	.286
1933	Homestead Grays	34	116		42	8	1	6		1	.362
1934	Pitt. Crawfords	50	190		56	**13**	4	**12**		0	.295
1935	Pitt. Crawfords	49	191		58	11	2	**13**		8	.304
1936	Pitt. Crawfords	23	75		27	3	0	**11**		0	.360
1937	Homestead Grays	12	42		21	0	**4**	7		0	.500
1938	Homestead Grays	18	60		21	2	0	4		1	.350
1939	Homestead Grays	27	72		24	2	2	**16**		0	.333
1940	Homestead Grays	1	6		1	0	0	0		0	.167
1942	Homestead Grays	40	125		43	6	1	**9**		3	**.344**
1943	Homestead Grays		**190**		**90**	**32**	**8**	**14**		0	**.474**
1944	Homestead Grays	48	165		57	8	5	**8**		2	.345
1945	Homestead Grays	**49**	161		64	6	4	9		0	.398
1946	Homestead Grays		119		43	7	5	**18**		0	.361
Negro League Totals			1820		644	110	45	141		17	.354

Bold = Led league

Notes
>Inducted into Hall of Fame (1972);
>Statistics are incomplete, but have been pieced together by diligent research;
>The Homestead Grays were based in Pittsburgh and Washington, D.C.;
>Won nine home run titles while playing just 11 full Negro League seasons;
>Played in Mexico in 1941 and hit league-leading 33 homers in 358 at-bats;
>Following the 1934 season, a team of Major League All-Stars played the Pittsburgh Crawfords, and Gibson hit 2 homers in one game off Dizzy Dean;
>Hall of Fame pitcher Walter Johnson on Gibson: "He hits the ball a mile. Throws like a rifle.";
>Hall of Fame catcher Roy Campanella on Gibson: "When I broke [into the Negro Leagues] in 1937 there were already a thousand legends about him; once you saw him play, you knew they were all true.";
>Passed away in January 1947, three months before Jackie Robinson broke the color barrier.

Juan Gonzalez (for more information, see pages 74–75)

Year	Team	G	AB	R	H	2B	3B	HR	RBI	SB	AVG
1989	Texas	24	60	6	9	3	0	1	7	0	.150
1990	Texas	25	90	11	26	7	1	4	12	0	.289
1991	Texas	142	545	78	144	34	1	27	102	4	.264
1992	Texas	155	584	77	152	24	2	**43**	109	0	.260
1993	Texas	140	536	105	166	33	1	**46**	118	4	.310
1994	Texas	107	422	57	116	18	4	19	85	6	.275
1995	Texas	90	352	57	104	20	2	27	82	0	.295
1996	Texas	134	541	89	170	33	2	47	144	2	.314
1997	Texas	133	533	87	158	24	3	42	131	0	.296
1998	Texas	154	606	110	193	**50**	2	45	**157**	2	.318
1999	Texas	144	562	114	183	36	1	39	128	3	.326
2000	Detroit	115	461	69	133	30	2	22	67	1	.289
2001	Cleveland	140	532	97	173	34	1	35	140	1	.325
2002	Texas	70	277	38	78	21	1	8	35	2	.282
2003	Texas	82	327	49	96	17	1	24	70	1	.294
Totals		1655	6428	1044	1901	384	24	429	1387	26	.296

Bold = Led league

Notes
>Three-time All Star (1993, 1998, 2001);
>Played in four postseason series, hitting .290 with 8 home runs in 62 at-bats, and is one of two players to homer in 4 consecutive games of a single postseason series (1996 ALDS), joining Jeffrey Leonard (1987 NLCS);
>Two-time American League Most Valuable Player (1996, 1998);
>All-time home run leader among players born in Puerto Rico, surpassing Orlando Cepeda (379);
>Joined Ken Griffey, Jr. as first players with three consecutive seasons with at least 130 RBI (1996–1998) since Vern Stephens (1948–1950);
>Second-most RBI at the All-Star break, with 101 in 1998 (Hank Greenberg had 103 in 1935);

Hank Greenberg (for more information, see pages 76–77)

Year	Team	G	AB	R	H	2B	3B	HR	RBI	SB	AVG
1930	Detroit	1	1	0	0	0	0	0	0	0	.000
1933	Detroit	117	449	59	135	33	3	12	87	6	.301
1934	Detroit	153	593	118	201	**63**	7	26	139	9	.339
1935	Detroit	152	619	121	203	46	16	**36**	**170**	4	.328
1936	Detroit	12	46	10	16	6	2	1	16	1	.348
1937	Detroit	154	594	137	200	49	14	40	183	8	.337
1938	Detroit	155	556	**144**	175	23	4	**58**	146	7	.315
1939	Detroit	138	500	112	156	42	7	33	112	8	.312
1940	Detroit	148	573	129	195	**50**	8	**41**	**150**	6	.340
1941	Detroit	19	67	12	18	5	1	2	12	1	.269
1945	Detroit	78	270	47	84	20	2	13	60	3	.311
1946	Detroit	142	523	91	145	29	5	**44**	**127**	5	.277
1947	Pittsburgh	125	402	71	100	13	2	25	74	0	.249
Totals		1394	5193	1051	1628	379	71	331	1276	58	.313

Bold = Led league

Notes
> Inducted into Hall of Fame (1956);
> Selected to five All-Star Games (1937–1940, 1945);
> Played in four World Series, hitting .318 with 5 homers and 22 RBI in 85 at-bats;
> Two-time American League Most Valuable Player award winner (1935, 1940);
> Set record with 103 RBI before the All-Star break (1935);
> Hit 58 home runs in 1938 to fall just 2 homers shy of Babe Ruth's record;
> Ranks second all-time (post-1900) to Lou Gehrig in career RBI per game (.92);
> Third-most RBI in a single season (183 in 1937), and joins Lou Gehrig as the only two players to have at least two seasons with at least 170 RBI;
> The Pirates built a short fence in left field and called it "Greenberg Gardens";
> Played only first base from 1933–1939, then only played left field in 1940, 1941, and 1945, until moving back to first base for final two seasons;
> Missed most of 1936 season with a broken wrist;
> Was in the army from May 1941 through July 1945, and came back to the Tigers and hit the pennant-clinching grand slam on the final day of the season;
> Had first pro tryout with New York Giants at age 18, but Giants manager John McGraw felt Greenberg was too clumsy and uncoordinated.

Ken Griffey, Jr. (for more information, see pages 40-41)

Year	Team	G	AB	R	H	2B	3B	HR	RBI	SB	AVG
1989	Seattle	127	455	61	120	23	0	16	61	16	.264
1990	Seattle	155	597	91	179	28	7	22	80	16	.300
1991	Seattle	154	548	76	179	42	1	22	100	18	.327
1992	Seattle	142	565	83	174	39	4	27	103	10	.308
1993	Seattle	156	582	113	180	38	3	45	109	17	.309
1994	Seattle	111	433	94	140	24	4	**40**	90	11	.323
1995	Seattle	72	260	52	67	7	0	17	42	4	.258
1996	Seattle	140	545	125	165	26	2	49	140	16	.303
1997	Seattle	157	608	**125**	185	34	3	**56**	**147**	15	.304
1998	Seattle	161	633	120	180	33	3	**56**	146	20	.284
1999	Seattle	160	606	123	173	26	3	**48**	134	24	.285
2000	Cincinnati	145	520	100	141	22	3	40	118	6	.271
2001	Cincinnati	111	364	57	104	20	2	22	65	2	.286
2002	Cincinnati	70	197	17	52	8	0	8	23	1	.264
2003	Cincinnati	53	166	34	41	12	1	13	26	1	.247
Totals		1914	7079	1271	2080	382	36	481	1384	177	.294

Bold = Led league

Notes
> Selected to start in 11 consecutive All-Star Games (1990–2000), and led the majors in fan voting five times;
> Played in three postseason series, hitting .305 with 6 home runs and 11 RBI and 59 at-bats;
> American League Most Valuable Player (1997);
> Youngest player to reach 400 homers (30 years, 141 days) and 450 homers (31 years, 261 days);
> Joins Babe Ruth and Lou Gehrig as only players with at least 140 RBI in three consecutive seasons;
> One of three players to hit 50 homers and steal 20 bases in a season (Willie Mays in 1955 and Brady Anderson in 1996);
> One of six players to hit at least 40 home runs in seven different seasons (Babe Ruth 11, Hank Aaron 8, Harmon Killebrew 8, Sammy Sosa 7, and Barry Bonds 7);
> Is one of six players to have hit 40 home runs in each league (Darrell Evans, Mark McGwire, David Justice, Shawn Green, and Jim Thome);
> Ranked second in both home runs (382, Mark McGwire had 405) and RBI (1,091, Albert Belle had 1,099) in the 1990s;

Vladimir Guerrero (for more information, see pages 16-17)

Year	Team	G	AB	R	H	2B	3B	HR	RBI	SB	AVG
1996	Montreal	9	27	2	5	0	0	1	1	0	.185
1997	Montreal	90	325	44	98	22	2	11	40	3	.302
1998	Montreal	159	623	108	202	37	7	38	109	11	.324
1999	Montreal	160	610	102	193	37	5	42	131	14	.316
2000	Montreal	154	571	101	197	28	11	44	123	9	.345
2001	Montreal	159	599	107	184	45	4	34	108	37	.307
2002	Montreal	161	614	106	**206**	37	2	39	111	40	.336
2003	Montreal	112	394	71	130	20	3	25	79	9	.330
Totals		1004	3763	641	1215	226	34	234	702	123	.323

Bold = Led league

Notes
>Appeared in four All-Star Games (1999–2002);
>At age 22, in 1998, hit 38 homers with 109 RBI and a .324 average—only Mel Ott and Joe DiMaggio had a season before turning 23 in which they matched or surpassed Guerrero's numbers in all three categories;
>One of five players to hit 30 homers, 100 RBI, and post a .300 average in three consecutive seasons before the age of 25 (1998–2000), along with Joe DiMaggio, Ted Williams, Jimmie Foxx, and Albert Pujols;
>Joined Lou Gehrig (1929–1937), Babe Ruth (1926–1932), Jimmie Foxx (1932–1936), and Frank Thomas (1993–1997) as the only players to hit .300 with 30 homers, 100 RBIs, and 100 runs scored in five consecutive seasons;
>Fifth player in history with consecutive 30-homer, 30-steal seasons, joining Willie Mays (1956–1957), Bobby Bonds (1977–1978), Ron Gant (1990–1991), and Barry Bonds (1995–1997);
>His 31-game hitting streak in 1999 was the longest hitting streak in the majors during the 1990s, and was the fourth-longest streak in 50 years (1949);
>In 2002, led the National League in hits and total bases, tied for first in outfield assists, finished second in intentional walks, third in average, fourth in steals, and fifth in home runs, RBI, and slugging percentage, sixth in runs, and seventh in on-base percentage;
>Played with his brother, Wilton, for four years (1998–2000, 2002) in Montreal.

Tony Gwynn (for more information, see pages 18-19)

Year	Team	G	AB	R	H	2B	3B	HR	RBI	SB	AVG
1982	San Diego	54	190	33	55	12	2	1	17	8	.289
1983	San Diego	86	304	34	94	12	2	1	37	7	.309
1984	San Diego	158	606	88	**213**	21	10	5	71	33	**.351**
1985	San Diego	154	622	90	197	29	5	6	46	14	.317
1986	San Diego	160	**642**	**107**	**211**	33	7	14	59	37	.329
1987	San Diego	157	589	119	**218**	36	13	7	54	56	**.370**
1988	San Diego	133	521	64	163	22	5	7	70	26	**.313**
1989	San Diego	158	604	82	**203**	27	7	4	62	40	**.336**
1990	San Diego	141	573	79	177	29	10	4	72	17	.309
1991	San Diego	134	530	69	168	27	11	4	62	8	.317
1992	San Diego	128	520	77	165	27	3	6	41	3	.317
1993	San Diego	122	489	70	175	41	3	7	59	14	.358
1994	San Diego	110	419	79	**165**	35	1	12	64	5	**.394**
1995	San Diego	135	535	82	**197**	33	1	9	90	17	**.368**
1996	San Diego	116	451	67	159	27	2	3	50	11	**.353**
1997	San Diego	149	592	97	**220**	49	2	17	119	12	**.372**
1998	San Diego	127	461	65	148	35	0	16	69	3	.321
1999	San Diego	111	411	59	139	27	0	10	62	7	.338
2000	San Diego	36	127	17	41	12	0	1	17	0	.323
2001	San Diego	71	102	5	33	9	1	1	17	1	.324
Totals		2440	9288	1383	3141	543	85	135	1138	319	.338

Bold = Led league

Notes
>15-time All Star (1984–1987, 1989–1999);
>Played in six postseason series, including two World Series in which he hit .371 with 1 home run and 3 RBI in 35 at-bats;
>Five-time National League Gold Glove award winner (1986, 1987, 1989–1991);
>Shares record for most National League batting titles (eight) with Honus Wagner;
>Only National Leaguer since 1900 to hit at least .300 for 16 consecutive seasons;
>Batted .394 in the strike-shortened 1994 season, the highest batting average since Ted Williams hit .406 in 1941;
>Owns highest career average (.338) by a player since Ted Williams (.344);
>Stole 5 bases in a game against Houston (September 20, 1986);
>Was the starting point guard on San Diego State's college basketball team.

Rickey Henderson (for more information, see pages 90-91)

Year	Team	G	AB	R	H	2B	3B	HR	RBI	SB	AVG
1979	Oakland	89	351	49	96	13	3	1	26	33	.274
1980	Oakland	158	591	111	179	22	4	9	53	**100**	.303
1981	Oakland	108	423	**89**	**135**	18	7	6	35	**56**	.319
1982	Oakland	149	536	119	143	24	4	10	51	**130**	.267
1983	Oakland	145	513	105	150	25	7	9	48	**108**	.292
1984	Oakland	142	502	113	147	27	4	16	58	**66**	.293
1985	N.Y. Yankees	143	547	**146**	172	28	5	24	72	**80**	.314
1986	N.Y. Yankees	153	608	**130**	160	31	5	28	74	**87**	.263
1987	N.Y. Yankees	95	358	78	104	17	3	17	37	41	.291
1988	N.Y. Yankees	140	554	118	169	30	2	6	50	**93**	.305
1989	N.Y. Yankees	65	235	**41**	58	13	1	3	22	**25**	.247
1989	Oakland	85	306	**72**	90	13	2	9	35	**52**	.294
1990	Oakland	136	489	**119**	159	33	3	28	61	**65**	.325
1991	Oakland	134	470	105	126	17	1	18	57	**58**	.268
1992	Oakland	117	396	77	112	18	3	15	46	48	.283
1993	Oakland	90	318	77	104	19	1	17	47	31	.327
1993	Toronto	44	163	37	35	3	1	4	12	22	.215
1994	Oakland	87	296	66	77	13	0	6	20	22	.260
1995	Oakland	112	407	67	122	31	1	9	54	32	.300
1996	San Diego	148	465	110	112	17	2	9	29	37	.241
1997	San Diego	88	288	63	79	11	0	6	27	29	.274
1997	Anaheim	32	115	21	21	3	0	2	7	16	.183
1998	Oakland	152	542	101	128	16	1	14	57	**66**	.236
1999	N.Y. Mets	121	438	89	138	30	0	12	42	37	.315
2000	N.Y. Mets	31	96	17	21	1	0	0	2	5	.219
2000	Seattle	92	324	58	77	13	2	4	30	31	.238
2001	San Diego	123	379	70	86	17	3	8	42	25	.227
2002	Boston	72	179	40	40	6	1	5	16	8	.223
2003	Los Angeles	30	72	7	15	1	0	2	5	3	.208
Totals		3081	10961	2295	3055	510	66	297	1115	1406	.279

Bold = Led league

Notes

> Selected to 10 All-Star games and won American League MVP award (1990);
> Played in 14 postseason series, including three World Series in which he hit .339 with 2 homers, 6 RBI, and 7 stolen bases in 56 at-bats;
> All-time leader in runs (2,295), stolen bases (1,406), and walks (2,190).

Rogers Hornsby (for more information, see pages 106-107)

Year	Team	G	AB	R	H	2B	3B	HR	RBI	SB	AVG
1915	St. Louis	18	57	5	14	2	0	0	4	0	.246
1916	St. Louis	139	495	63	155	17	15	6	65	17	.313
1917	St. Louis	145	523	86	171	24	**17**	8	66	17	.327
1918	St. Louis	115	416	51	117	19	11	5	60	8	.281
1919	St. Louis	138	512	68	163	15	9	8	71	17	.318
1920	St. Louis	149	589	96	**218**	**44**	20	9	**94**	12	**.370**
1921	St. Louis	**154**	592	**131**	**235**	**44**	**18**	21	**126**	13	**.397**
1922	St. Louis	154	623	**141**	**250**	**46**	14	**42**	**152**	17	**.401**
1923	St. Louis	107	424	89	163	32	10	17	83	3	**.384**
1924	St. Louis	143	536	**121**	**227**	**43**	14	25	94	5	**.424**
1925	St. Louis	138	504	133	203	41	10	**39**	**143**	5	**.403**
1926	St. Louis	134	527	96	167	34	5	11	93	3	.317
1927	N.Y. Giants	**155**	568	**133**	205	32	9	26	125	9	.361
1928	Boston Braves	140	486	99	188	42	7	21	94	5	**.387**
1929	Chicago Cubs	**156**	602	**156**	229	47	8	39	149	2	.380
1930	Chicago Cubs	42	104	15	32	5	1	2	18	0	.308
1931	Chicago Cubs	100	357	64	118	37	1	16	90	1	.331
1932	Chicago Cubs	19	58	10	13	2	0	1	7	0	.224
1933	St. Louis	46	83	9	27	6	0	2	21	1	.325
1933	St. L. Browns	11	9	2	3	1	0	1	2	0	.333
1934	St. L. Browns	24	23	2	7	2	0	1	11	0	.304
1935	St. L. Browns	10	24	1	5	3	0	0	3	0	.208
1936	St. L. Browns	2	5	1	2	0	0	0	2	0	.400
1937	St. L. Browns	20	56	7	18	3	0	1	11	0	.321
Totals		2259	8173	1579	2930	541	169	301	1584	135	.358

Bold = Led league

Notes
>Inducted into Hall of Fame (1942);
>Played in two World Series (1926, 1929), hitting .245 with 5 RBI in 49 at-bats;
>Two-time National League MVP (1925, 1929);
>He and Ted Williams are only two players with two Triple Crowns (1922, 1925);
>Owns second-best average of all time, and has best batting average in a four-year period (.404 from 1922–1925) and a five-year window (.402 from 1921–1925);
>Set National League record for most consecutive batting titles (six, 1920–1925);
>He was often a player-manager during 1925–1937.

Reggie Jackson (for more information, see pages 42-43)

Year	Team	G	AB	R	H	2B	3B	HR	RBI	SB	AVG
1967	Kansas City A's	35	118	13	21	4	4	1	6	1	.178
1968	Oakland	154	553	82	138	13	6	29	74	14	.250
1969	Oakland	152	549	**123**	151	36	3	47	118	13	.275
1970	Oakland	149	426	57	101	21	2	23	66	26	.237
1971	Oakland	150	567	87	157	29	3	32	80	16	.277
1972	Oakland	135	499	72	132	25	2	25	75	9	.265
1973	Oakland	151	539	**99**	158	28	2	**32**	**117**	22	.293
1974	Oakland	148	506	90	146	25	1	29	93	25	.289
1975	Oakland	157	593	91	150	39	3	**36**	104	17	.253
1976	Baltimore	134	498	84	138	27	2	27	91	28	.277
1977	N.Y. Yankees	146	525	93	150	39	2	32	110	17	.286
1978	N.Y. Yankees	139	511	82	140	13	5	27	97	14	.274
1979	N.Y. Yankees	131	465	78	138	24	2	29	89	9	.297
1980	N.Y. Yankees	143	514	94	154	22	4	**41**	111	1	.300
1981	N.Y. Yankees	94	334	33	79	17	1	15	54	0	.237
1982	California	153	530	92	146	17	1	**39**	101	4	.275
1983	California	116	397	43	77	14	1	14	49	0	.194
1984	California	143	525	67	117	17	2	25	81	8	.223
1985	California	143	460	64	116	27	0	27	85	1	.252
1986	California	132	419	65	101	12	2	18	58	1	.241
1987	Oakland	115	336	42	74	14	1	15	43	2	.220
Totals		2820	9864	1551	2584	463	49	563	1702	228	.262

Bold = Led league

Notes
> First-ballot Hall of Fame inductee (1993);
> Played in 14 All-Star Games (1969, 1971–1975, 1977–1984);
> Participated in postseason play 11 times, including five World Series (1973–1974, 1977–1978, 1981), hitting .357 with 10 home runs in 98 career at-bats.
> Earned the nickname "Mr. October" by being the only player to win two World Series MVP awards (1973 and 1977, when he tied a record with 3 homers in a game), and owns best slugging percentage in World Series play (.755);
> 1973 American League MVP;
> Ranks eighth all-time in homers (563) and first in strikeouts (2,597);
> The Mets drafted catcher Steve Chilcott with the first pick of the 1967 draft, and the A's selected Jackson with the next pick. Chilcott never made it to the majors.

Derek Jeter (for more information, see pages 20-21)

Year	Team	G	AB	R	H	2B	3B	HR	RBI	SB	AVG
1995	N.Y. Yankees	15	48	5	12	4	1	0	7	0	.250
1996	N.Y. Yankees	157	582	104	183	25	6	10	78	14	.314
1997	N.Y. Yankees	159	654	116	190	31	7	10	70	23	.291
1998	N.Y. Yankees	149	626	**127**	203	25	8	19	84	30	.324
1999	N.Y. Yankees	158	627	134	**219**	37	9	24	102	19	.349
2000	N.Y. Yankees	148	593	119	201	31	4	15	73	22	.339
2001	N.Y. Yankees	150	614	110	191	35	3	21	74	27	.311
2002	N.Y. Yankees	157	644	124	191	26	0	18	75	32	.297
2003	N.Y. Yankees	119	482	87	156	25	3	10	52	11	.324
Totals		1212	4870	926	1546	239	41	127	615	178	.317

Bold = Led league

Notes
>Five-time All Star (1998–2002);
>Played in eight postseason series, including six World Series in which he hit .302 (including four Series with averages above .345) with 3 home runs and 8 RBI, in 129 at-bats; was 2000 World Series MVP after hitting .409 with 2 home runs in 22 at-bats;
>American League Rookie of the Year (1996);
>Ranks fifth in Yankees history (minimum 500 games) with a .317 career average, trailing only Babe Ruth (.349), Lou Gehrig (.340), Earle Combs (.325), and Joe DiMaggio (.325);
>Ranks fifth among active players in career batting average, trailing Todd Helton, Nomar Garciaparra, Vladimir Guerrero, and Mike Piazza;
>In 2003, finished third in batting average;
>In 2002, ranked in the top ten in: runs (third), at-bats (fourth), and hits (seventh);
>In 1999, ranked in the American League top ten in: hits (first), batting average (second), runs (second), and at-bats (sixth);
>In 1998, led league in runs, and ranked high in hits (third), and average (fifth);
>Yankees first-round selection (sixth overall) in the 1992 draft.

Jeff Kent (for more information, see pages 78-79)

Year	Team	G	AB	R	H	2B	3B	HR	RBI	SB	AVG
1992	Toronto	65	192	36	46	13	1	8	35	2	.240
1992	N.Y. Mets	37	113	16	27	8	1	3	15	0	.239
1993	N.Y. Mets	140	496	65	134	24	0	21	80	4	.270
1994	N.Y. Mets	107	415	53	121	24	5	14	68	1	.292
1995	N.Y. Mets	125	472	65	131	22	3	20	65	3	.278
1996	N.Y. Mets	89	335	45	97	20	1	9	39	4	.290
1996	Cleveland	39	102	16	27	7	0	3	16	2	.265
1997	San Francisco	155	580	90	145	38	2	29	121	11	.250
1998	San Francisco	137	526	94	156	37	3	31	128	9	.297
1999	San Francisco	138	511	86	148	40	2	23	101	13	.290
2000	San Francisco	159	587	114	196	41	7	33	125	12	.334
2001	San Francisco	159	607	84	181	49	6	22	106	7	.298
2002	San Francisco	152	623	102	195	42	2	37	108	5	.313
2003	Houston	130	505	77	150	39	1	22	93	6	.297
Totals		**1632**	**6064**	**943**	**1754**	**404**	**34**	**275**	**1100**	**79**	**.289**

Notes

>Selected to three All-Star Games (1999–2001);

>Played in six postseason series, including 2002 World Series in which he hit .276 with 3 home runs and 7 RBI in 29 at-bats, and shares the Division Series record for most home runs in a game (2, against Florida in 1997);

>National League Most Valuable Player award winner (2000), and finished in the top ten in voting three other times;

>In 1997, was first second baseman with 120 RBI since Jackie Robinson (1949);

>Joins Rogers Hornsby as the only second basemen in history with multiple 120 RBI seasons, and joins Hornsby as the only second basemen with at least three 30-homer campaigns;

>Is only the fourth player in Giants history to post at least six consecutive 100-RBI seasons, joining Hall of Famers Bill Terry (1927–1932), Mel Ott (1929–1936), and Willie Mays (1959–1966);

>Only the third player to record three consecutive 100-RBI seasons as a second baseman, joining Charlie Gehringer and Bobby Doerr.

Mickey Mantle (for more information, see pages 108-109)

Year	Team	G	AB	R	H	2B	3B	HR	RBI	SB	AVG
1951	N.Y. Yankees	96	341	61	91	11	5	13	65	8	.267
1952	N.Y. Yankees	142	549	94	171	37	7	23	87	4	.311
1953	N.Y. Yankees	127	461	105	136	24	3	21	92	8	.295
1954	N.Y. Yankees	146	543	**129**	163	17	12	27	102	5	.300
1955	N.Y. Yankees	147	517	121	158	25	**11**	**37**	99	8	.306
1956	N.Y. Yankees	150	533	**132**	188	22	5	52	**130**	10	**.353**
1957	N.Y. Yankees	144	474	**121**	173	28	6	34	94	16	.365
1958	N.Y. Yankees	150	519	**127**	158	21	1	**42**	97	18	.304
1959	N.Y. Yankees	144	541	104	154	23	4	31	75	21	.285
1960	N.Y. Yankees	153	527	**119**	145	17	6	**40**	94	14	.275
1961	N.Y. Yankees	153	514	**132**	163	16	6	54	128	12	.317
1962	N.Y. Yankees	123	377	96	121	15	1	30	89	9	.321
1963	N.Y. Yankees	65	172	40	54	8	0	15	35	2	.314
1964	N.Y. Yankees	143	465	92	141	25	2	35	111	6	.303
1965	N.Y. Yankees	122	361	44	92	12	1	19	46	4	.255
1966	N.Y. Yankees	108	333	40	96	12	1	23	56	1	.288
1967	N.Y. Yankees	144	440	63	108	17	0	22	55	1	.245
1968	N.Y. Yankees	144	435	57	103	14	1	18	54	6	.237
Totals		**2401**	**8102**	**1677**	**2415**	**344**	**72**	**536**	**1509**	**153**	**.298**

Bold = Led league

Notes

>First-ballot Hall of Fame inductee (1974);
>Played in 16 All-Star Games (1953–1962, 1964, 1967–1968);
>Participated in 12 World Series (1951–1953, 1955–1958, 1960–1964), hitting .257 with World Series records in home runs (18), RBI (40), and runs (42) in 230 at-bats;
>Three-time American League MVP (1956, 1957, 1962);
>American League Triple Crown (1956), and Gold Glove winner (1962);
>The first switch-hitter with tremendous power from both sides of the plate, his 565-foot home run in 1953 began the trend of measuring long homers;
>Holds Yankees record for games played (2,401);
>Was incredibly fast but suffered numerous injuries, beginning in the 1951 World Series when he tore up his knee;
>Named for catcher Mickey Cochrane, who was later inducted into Hall of Fame.

Willie Mays (for more information, see pages 64-65)

Year	Team	G	AB	R	H	2B	3B	HR	RBI	SB	AVG
1951	N.Y. Giants	121	464	59	127	22	5	20	68	7	.274
1952	N.Y. Giants	34	127	17	30	2	4	4	23	4	.236
1954	N.Y. Giants	151	565	119	195	33	**13**	41	110	8	**.345**
1955	N.Y. Giants	152	580	123	185	18	**13**	**51**	127	24	.319
1956	N.Y. Giants	152	578	101	171	27	8	36	84	**40**	.296
1957	N.Y. Giants	152	585	112	195	26	**20**	35	97	**38**	.333
1958	San Francisco	152	600	**121**	208	33	11	29	96	**31**	.347
1959	San Francisco	151	575	125	180	43	5	34	104	**27**	.313
1960	San Francisco	153	595	107	**190**	29	12	29	103	25	.319
1961	San Francisco	154	572	**129**	176	32	3	40	123	18	.308
1962	San Francisco	162	621	130	189	36	5	**49**	141	18	.304
1963	San Francisco	157	596	115	187	32	7	38	103	8	.314
1964	San Francisco	157	578	121	171	21	9	**47**	111	19	.296
1965	San Francisco	157	558	118	177	21	3	**52**	112	9	.317
1966	San Francisco	152	552	99	159	29	4	37	103	5	.288
1967	San Francisco	141	486	83	128	22	2	22	70	6	.263
1968	San Francisco	148	498	84	144	20	5	23	79	12	.289
1969	San Francisco	117	403	64	114	17	3	13	58	6	.283
1970	San Francisco	139	478	94	139	15	2	28	83	5	.291
1971	San Francisco	136	417	82	113	24	5	18	61	23	.271
1972	San Francisco	19	49	8	9	2	0	0	3	3	.184
1972	N.Y. Mets	69	195	27	52	9	1	8	19	1	.267
1973	N.Y. Mets	66	209	24	44	10	0	6	25	1	.211
Totals		2992	10881	2062	3283	523	140	660	1903	338	.302

Bold = Led league

Notes
>First-ballot Hall of Fame inductee (1979);
>Played in a record 24 consecutive All-Star Games (1954–1973);
>Participated in postseason play five times, including four World Series (1951, 1954, 1962, 1973), hitting .239 with 6 RBI in 71 at-bats;
>Two-time National League MVP (1954, 1965), and finished in the top five in voting 9 times, and missed 1952 and 1953 seasons while serving in the Army.
>Won 12 consecutive National League Gold Glove awards (1957–1968) in outfield;
>Considered one of the best players of all time, Mays ranks in the top ten in: home runs (third), runs (sixth), RBI (ninth), and games (ninth).

Mark McGwire (for more information, see pages 46-47)

Year	Team	G	AB	R	H	2B	3B	HR	RBI	SB	AVG
1986	Oakland	18	53	10	10	1	0	3	9	0	.189
1987	Oakland	151	557	97	161	28	4	**49**	118	1	.289
1988	Oakland	155	550	87	143	22	1	32	99	0	.260
1989	Oakland	143	490	74	113	17	0	33	95	1	.231
1990	Oakland	156	523	87	123	16	0	39	108	2	.235
1991	Oakland	154	483	62	97	22	0	22	75	2	.201
1992	Oakland	139	467	87	125	22	0	42	104	0	.268
1993	Oakland	27	84	16	28	6	0	9	24	0	.333
1994	Oakland	47	135	26	34	3	0	9	25	0	.252
1995	Oakland	104	317	75	87	13	0	39	90	1	.274
1996	Oakland	130	423	104	132	21	0	**52**	113	0	.312
1997	Oakland	105	366	48	104	24	0	34	81	1	.284
1997	St. Louis	51	174	38	44	3	0	24	42	2	.253
1998	St. Louis	155	509	130	152	21	0	**70**	147	1	.299
1999	St. Louis	153	521	118	145	21	1	**65**	**147**	0	.278
2000	St. Louis	89	236	60	72	8	0	32	73	1	.305
2001	St. Louis	97	299	48	56	4	0	29	64	0	.187
Totals		1874	6187	1167	1626	252	6	583	1414	12	.263

Bold = Led league

Notes
>Selected to 12 All-Star teams (1987–1992, 1995–2000);
>Participated in 10 postseason series, including three World Series (1988–1990), hitting .187 with 1 home run in 48 at-bats;
>American League Rookie of the Year (1987) and Gold Glove winner (1990);
>Broke Roger Maris' single-season home run record with his 62nd home run on September 8, 1998, in game 145, against Steve Trachsel of the Chicago Cubs;
>Hit a home run every 9.4 at-bats to break Babe Ruth's record (11.8 at-bats), and in his final seven seasons, hit 345 homers in 2,845 at-bats (8.2 at-bats);
>Ranked sixth all-time in home runs (583);
>Set rookie record for homers in a season (49 in 1987);
>Led the major leagues in homers four consecutive seasons, but did not lead a particular league in 1997 because he hit 58 home runs between Oakland (American League) and St. Louis (National League).

Stan Musial (for more information, see pages 22-23)

Year	Team	G	AB	R	H	2B	3B	HR	RBI	SB	AVG
1941	St. Louis	12	47	8	20	4	0	1	7	1	.426
1942	St. Louis	140	467	87	147	32	10	10	72	6	.315
1943	St. Louis	**157**	617	108	**220**	48	**20**	13	81	9	**.357**
1944	St. Louis	146	568	112	**197**	51	14	12	94	7	.347
1946	St. Louis	156	**624**	**124**	**228**	50	**20**	16	103	7	**.365**
1947	St. Louis	149	587	113	183	30	13	19	95	4	.312
1948	St. Louis	155	611	**135**	**230**	**46**	**18**	39	**131**	7	**.376**
1949	St. Louis	**157**	612	128	**207**	41	**13**	36	123	3	.338
1950	St. Louis	146	555	105	192	41	7	28	109	5	**.346**
1951	St. Louis	152	578	**124**	205	30	**12**	32	108	4	**.355**
1952	St. Louis	**154**	578	**105**	**194**	42	6	21	91	7	**.336**
1953	St. Louis	157	593	127	200	**53**	9	30	113	3	.337
1954	St. Louis	153	591	**120**	195	**41**	9	35	126	1	.330
1955	St. Louis	**154**	562	97	179	30	5	33	108	5	.319
1956	St. Louis	156	594	87	184	33	6	27	**109**	2	.310
1957	St. Louis	134	502	82	176	38	3	29	102	1	**.351**
1958	St. Louis	135	472	64	159	35	2	17	62	0	.337
1959	St. Louis	115	341	37	87	13	2	14	44	0	.255
1960	St. Louis	116	331	49	91	17	1	17	63	1	.275
1961	St. Louis	123	372	46	107	22	4	15	70	0	.288
1962	St. Louis	135	433	57	143	18	1	19	82	3	.330
1963	St. Louis	124	337	34	86	10	2	12	58	2	.255
Totals		3026	10972	1949	3630	725	177	475	1951	78	.331

Bold = Led league

Notes
>First-ballot Hall of Fame inductee (1969);
>Played in 24 All-Star Games (1943–1944, 1946–1963);
>Participated in four World Series (1942–1944, 1946), hitting .256 with 1 home run in 86 at-bats;
>Three-time National League MVP (1943, 1946, 1948), and finished in the top five in voting 9 times;
>Ranks in the top ten all time in: doubles (third), hits (fourth), RBI (fifth), games (sixth), runs (eighth), and at-bats (ninth);
>First player to hit 5 home runs in a doubleheader (May 2, 1954);
>Had a 33–13 record as a minor league pitcher before suffering a shoulder injury while making a diving catch.

Rafael Palmeiro (for more information, see pages 48-49)

Year	Team	G	AB	R	H	2B	3B	HR	RBI	SB	AVG
1986	Chicago Cubs	22	73	9	18	4	0	3	12	1	.247
1987	Chicago Cubs	84	221	32	61	15	1	14	30	2	.276
1988	Chicago Cubs	152	580	75	178	41	5	8	53	12	.307
1989	Texas	156	559	76	154	23	4	8	64	4	.275
1990	Texas	154	598	72	**191**	35	6	14	89	3	.319
1991	Texas	159	631	115	203	**49**	3	26	88	4	.322
1992	Texas	159	608	84	163	27	4	22	85	2	.268
1993	Texas	160	597	**124**	176	40	2	37	105	22	.295
1994	Baltimore	111	436	82	139	32	0	23	76	7	.319
1995	Baltimore	143	554	89	172	30	2	39	104	3	.310
1996	Baltimore	162	626	110	181	40	2	39	142	8	.289
1997	Baltimore	158	614	95	156	24	2	38	110	5	.254
1998	Baltimore	162	619	98	183	36	1	43	121	11	.296
1999	Texas	158	565	96	183	30	1	47	148	2	.324
2000	Texas	158	565	102	163	29	3	39	120	2	.288
2001	Texas	160	600	98	164	33	0	47	123	1	.273
2002	Texas	155	546	99	149	34	0	43	105	2	.273
2003	Texas	154	561	92	146	21	2	38	112	2	.260
Totals		**2567**	**9553**	**1548**	**2780**	**543**	**38**	**528**	**1687**	**93**	**.291**

Bold = Led league

Notes

>Four-time All Star (1988, 1991, 1998, 1999);
>Played in five postseason series, hitting .244 with 4 home runs in 82 at-bats;
>Three-time American League Gold Glove winner (1997–1999);
>First player in Major League history to hit at least 38 home runs in nine consecutive seasons (1995–2003);
>Tied with Jimmie Foxx and Sammy Sosa for most consecutive seasons with at least 35 home runs and 100 RBI (nine, 1995–2003);
>Ranks thirteenth on career home run list;
>One of four players to have hit at least 45 homers at age 36 or older (2001), joining Babe Ruth, Hank Aaron, and Barry Bonds;
>One of five players to have hit at least 40 home runs with different teams in consecutive seasons (1998–1999);
>148 RBI (1999) were the most by a lefthanded hitter since Ted Williams (1949);
>Born in Cuba, and family moved to America in 1971 when Palmeiro was seven.

Mike Piazza (for more information, see pages 24–25)

Year	Team	G	AB	R	H	2B	3B	HR	RBI	SB	AVG
1992	Los Angeles	21	69	5	16	3	0	1	7	0	.232
1993	Los Angeles	149	547	81	174	24	2	35	112	3	.318
1994	Los Angeles	107	405	64	129	18	0	24	92	1	.319
1995	Los Angeles	112	434	82	150	17	0	32	93	1	.346
1996	Los Angeles	148	547	87	184	16	0	36	105	0	.336
1997	Los Angeles	152	556	104	201	32	1	40	124	5	.362
1998	Los Angeles	37	149	20	42	5	0	9	30	0	.282
1998	Florida	5	18	1	5	0	1	0	5	0	.278
1998	N.Y. Mets	109	394	67	137	33	0	23	76	1	.348
1999	N.Y. Mets	141	534	100	162	25	0	40	124	2	.303
2000	N.Y. Mets	136	482	90	156	26	0	38	113	4	.324
2001	N.Y. Mets	141	503	81	151	29	0	36	94	0	.300
2002	N.Y. Mets	135	478	69	134	23	2	33	98	0	.280
2003	N.Y. Mets	68	234	37	67	13	0	11	34	0	.286
Totals		1461	5350	888	1708	264	6	358	1107	17	.319

Bold = Led league

Notes
>Selected to 10 consecutive All-Star teams (1993–2002);
>Played in seven postseason series, including one World Series in which he hit
 .273 with 2 home runs and 4 RBI in 22 at-bats;
>National League Rookie of the Year (1993);
>Finished in the top four in National League Most Valuable Player voting four
 times (fourth in 1995, second in 1996 and 1997, and third in 2000);
>Set record for most consecutive 20-homer seasons by a catcher (10);
>Second in home runs hit by a catcher (346), trailing Carlton Fisk by 5 homers;
>Hit at least 30 homers eight consecutive years (1995–2002)—no other catcher has
 hit at least 30 home runs in more than two consecutive years;
>Set record for most homers hit by a rookie catcher (35 in 1993);
>Was the Dodgers' sixty-second round draft choice, and 1,390th overall pick, in
 the 1988 draft.

Albert Pujols (for more information, see pages 26-27)

Year	Team	G	AB	R	H	2B	3B	HR	RBI	SB	AVG
2001	St. Louis	161	590	112	194	47	4	37	130	1	.329
2002	St. Louis	157	590	118	185	40	2	34	127	2	.314
2003	St. Louis	157	591	**137**	**212**	**51**	1	43	124	5	**.359**
Totals		475	1771	367	591	138	7	114	381	8	.334

Bold = Led league

Notes

>Two-time All Star (2001, 2003);

>Played in three postseason series, hitting .213 with 2 home runs and 7 RBI in 47 at-bats;

>National League Rookie of the Year (2001), becoming just the seventh unanimous selection in league history;

>Finished in the top four in National League Most Valuable Player award voting each of his first three seasons (2001–2003);

>Set National League rookie records for RBI (130), extra-base hits (88), and total bases (360) in 2001;

>First National League rookie ever to hit at least .300 with 30 home runs, 100 RBI, and 100 runs scored, and is the first player ever to reach those statistics in each of his first two and three major league seasons, as well;

>Tied for most homers in history in first three seasons (Ralph Kiner, Mark McGwire);

>First Cardinals rookie to lead club in the Triple Crown categories (batting average, homers, RBI) since Rogers Hornsby in 1916;

>In 2001, became first Cardinals player to lead club in homers, RBI, batting average, and runs scored—and he turned the trick again in both 2002 and 2003;

>In 2001, became the first player ever to make 30 starts at four different positions in a season (third base 52, left field 37, right field 33, first base 31);

>Had only played one season in the minors, and not above Class A, and would have begun the 2001 season in the minors, but Bobby Bonilla was placed on the disabled list with a strained left hamstring and Pujols started in left field on opening day and wound up missing just one game the entire season;

>Born in Dominican Republic and moved to Kansas City with father at age 16.

Manny Ramirez (for more information, see pages 80-81)

Year	Team	G	AB	R	H	2B	3B	HR	RBI	SB	AVG
1993	Cleveland	22	53	5	9	1	0	2	5	0	.170
1994	Cleveland	91	290	51	78	22	0	17	60	4	.269
1995	Cleveland	137	484	85	149	26	1	31	107	6	.308
1996	Cleveland	152	550	94	170	45	3	33	112	8	.309
1997	Cleveland	150	561	99	184	40	0	26	88	2	.328
1998	Cleveland	150	571	108	168	35	2	45	145	5	.294
1999	Cleveland	147	522	131	174	34	3	44	**165**	2	.333
2000	Cleveland	118	439	92	154	34	2	38	122	1	.351
2001	Boston	142	529	93	162	33	2	41	125	0	.306
2002	Boston	120	436	84	152	31	0	33	107	0	**.349**
2003	Boston	154	569	117	185	36	1	37	104	3	.325
Totals		1383	5004	959	1585	337	14	347	1140	31	.317

Bold = Led league

Notes
>Selected to seven All-Star Games (1995, 1998-2003);
>Played in six postseason series, including two World Series (1995, 1997) in which he hit .182 with 3 home runs and 8 RBI in 44 at-bats, and is tied for fifth all-time with 16 postseason homers, trailing Bernie Williams (19), Mickey Mantle (18), and Reggie Jackson (18). Jim Thome also has 16;
>First player since 1938 (Jimmie Foxx) with at least 160 RBI (165 in 1999);
>Second player in history to hit 8 home runs in a five-game stretch (September 15–19, 1998), matching the feat of Frank Howard (1968);
>Has hit the second-most grand slams (15) among active players (trailing Robin Ventura, 16);
>The 15 grand slams are the most-ever by a Latin-born player;
>Has the sixth highest career batting average among active players with at least 3,000 at-bats (trailing Todd Helton, Nomar Garciaparra, Vladimir Guerrero, Mike Piazza, and Derek Jeter);
>Third player in Red Sox history to hit at least 40 homers in his first season with the club;
>In September 2002, became first Red Sox player to have at least 30 RBI in September since Jim Rice (1980);
>Born in the Dominican Republic and attended high school in the Bronx, N.Y.

Frank Robinson (for more information, see pages 110-111)

Year	Team	G	AB	R	H	2B	3B	HR	RBI	SB	AVG
1956	Cincinnati	152	572	**122**	166	27	6	38	83	8	.290
1957	Cincinnati	150	611	97	197	29	5	29	75	10	.322
1958	Cincinnati	148	554	90	149	25	6	31	83	10	.269
1959	Cincinnati	146	540	106	168	31	4	36	125	18	.311
1960	Cincinnati	139	464	86	138	33	6	31	83	13	.297
1961	Cincinnati	153	545	117	176	32	7	37	124	22	.323
1962	Cincinnati	162	609	**134**	208	**51**	2	39	136	18	.342
1963	Cincinnati	140	482	79	125	19	3	21	91	26	.259
1964	Cincinnati	156	568	103	174	38	6	29	96	23	.306
1965	Cincinnati	156	582	109	172	33	5	33	113	13	.296
1966	Baltimore	155	576	**122**	182	34	2	**49**	**122**	8	**.316**
1967	Baltimore	129	479	83	149	23	7	30	94	2	.311
1968	Baltimore	130	421	69	113	27	1	15	52	11	.268
1969	Baltimore	148	539	111	166	19	5	32	100	9	.308
1970	Baltimore	132	471	88	144	24	1	25	78	2	.306
1971	Baltimore	133	455	82	128	16	2	28	99	3	.281
1972	Los Angeles	103	342	41	86	6	1	19	59	2	.251
1973	California	147	534	85	142	29	0	30	97	1	.266
1974	California	129	427	75	107	26	2	20	63	5	.251
1974	Cleveland	15	50	6	10	1	1	2	5	0	.200
1975	Cleveland	49	118	19	28	5	0	9	24	0	.237
1976	Cleveland	36	67	5	15	0	0	3	10	0	.224
Totals		2808	10006	1829	2943	528	72	586	1812	204	.294

Bold = Led league

Notes
>First-ballot Hall of Fame inductee (1982);
>Played in 11 All-Star Games;
>Participated in five World Series (1961, 1966, 1969–1971), hitting .250 with 8 home run in 92 at-bats, and was 1966 World Series MVP with 2 homers in 14 at-bats;
>First player to win MVP award in both leagues (National, 1961; American, 1966)
>National League Rookie of the Year (1956) and Gold Glove winner (1958);
>Won American League Triple Crown (1966), the only time he led the league in any of the three categories during his career;
>Ranks fifth all-time in career home runs (586);
>Became first African-American manager (Cleveland, 1975–1977).

Jackie Robinson (for more information, see pages 92-93)

Year	Team	G	AB	R	H	2B	3B	HR	RBI	SB	AVG
1947	Brooklyn	151	590	125	175	31	5	12	48	**29**	.297
1948	Brooklyn	147	574	108	170	38	8	12	85	22	.296
1949	Brooklyn	156	593	122	203	38	12	16	124	**37**	**.342**
1950	Brooklyn	144	518	99	170	39	4	14	81	12	.328
1951	Brooklyn	153	548	106	185	33	7	19	88	25	.338
1952	Brooklyn	149	510	104	157	17	3	19	75	24	.308
1953	Brooklyn	136	484	109	159	34	7	12	95	17	.329
1954	Brooklyn	124	386	62	120	22	4	15	59	7	.311
1955	Brooklyn	105	317	51	81	6	2	8	36	12	.256
1956	Brooklyn	117	357	61	98	15	2	10	43	12	.275
Totals		1382	4877	947	1518	273	54	137	734	197	.311

Bold = Led league

Notes

> First African-American Hall of Fame inductee (1962);
> Played in six All-Star Games (1949–1954);
> Participated in six World Series (1947, 1949, 1952, 1953, 1955, 1956), hitting .234 with 2 home runs, 12 RBI, and 6 steals in 137 at-bats;
> National League MVP (1949) and National League Rookie of the Year (1947);
> He stole home 19 times, the most by anyone who played after 1940;
> Robinson served as a lieutenant in World War II, and played for the Kansas City Monarchs in the Negro Leagues prior to signing with the Dodgers in 1945. The Dodgers sent him to play in Montreal, and he led the league in average and runs scored en route to a championship;
> In a poll after the 1947 season, he was second only to Bing Crosby as the most popular man in America;
> Played shortstop in the Negro Leagues, and played first base, second base, third base, and outfield for the Dodgers;
> After the 1956 season, the Dodgers traded him to the Giants, but Robinson retired at the age of 37 instead of joining the long-time crosstown rivals;
> His uniform number, 42, has been retired by all 30 Major League teams;
> A four-sport star at UCLA, he averaged over 11 yards per carry as a football running back, in basketball he led the conference in scoring for two years, and won the 1940 NCAA long-jump title in track, in addition to playing baseball.

Alex Rodriguez (for more information, see pages 50-51)

Year	Team	G	AB	R	H	2B	3B	HR	RBI	SB	AVG
1994	Seattle	17	54	4	11	0	0	0	2	3	.204
1995	Seattle	48	142	15	33	6	2	5	19	4	.232
1996	Seattle	146	601	**141**	215	**54**	1	36	123	15	**.358**
1997	Seattle	141	587	100	176	40	3	23	84	29	.300
1998	Seattle	161	**686**	123	**213**	35	5	42	124	46	.310
1999	Seattle	129	502	110	143	25	0	42	111	21	.285
2000	Seattle	148	554	134	175	34	2	41	132	15	.316
2001	Texas	**162**	632	**133**	201	34	1	**52**	135	18	.318
2002	Texas	**162**	624	125	187	27	2	**57**	**142**	9	.300
2003	Texas	161	607	**124**	181	30	6	**47**	118	17	.298
Totals		1275	4989	1009	1535	285	22	345	990	177	.308

Bold = Led league

Notes
>Selected to seven All-Star Games (1996–1998, 2000–2003);
>Played in five postseason series, hitting .340 with 3 home runs and 8 RBI in 53 at-bats;
>Finished in the top six in American League Most Valuable Player voting five times (1996, 2000–03);
>Won Gold Glove award (2002);
>Second all-time with six consecutive 40-homer seasons, trailing Babe Ruth (7);
>In 1998, became just the third player to hit 40 home runs and steal 40 bases in the same season, joining Jose Canseco (1988) and Barry Bonds (1996);
>Set single-season record for home runs by a shortstop in 2001 (52), and surpassed that mark in 2002 (57);
>Established American League record with 109 home runs in back-to-back seasons (2001–2002);
>With 57 homers in 2002, became the second shortstop to lead the majors in home runs (Ernie Banks did it twice, in 1958 and 1960);
>In 2002, became the fourth shortstop to lead the majors in RBI (Honus Wagner in 1901 and 1908, Vern Stephens in 1949 and 1950, and Ernie Banks in 1958 and 1959);
>First shortstop to post six consecutive 100-RBI seasons (1998–2003);
>In 2001, at age 26, became the sixth youngest player to have a 50-homer season;
>In 1996, at age 21, became the third youngest player to win a batting title (Ty Cobb in 1907 and Al Kaline in 1955).

Pete Rose (for more information, see pages 28-29)

Year	Team	G	AB	R	H	2B	3B	HR	RBI	SB	AVG
1963	Cincinnati	157	623	101	170	25	9	6	41	13	.273
1964	Cincinnati	136	516	64	139	13	2	4	34	4	.269
1965	Cincinnati	162	**670**	117	**209**	35	11	11	81	8	.312
1966	Cincinnati	156	654	97	205	38	5	16	70	4	.313
1967	Cincinnati	148	585	86	176	32	8	12	76	11	.301
1968	Cincinnati	149	626	94	**210**	42	6	10	49	3	**.335**
1969	Cincinnati	156	627	**120**	218	33	11	16	82	7	**.348**
1970	Cincinnati	159	649	120	**205**	37	9	15	52	12	.316
1971	Cincinnati	160	632	86	192	27	4	13	44	13	.304
1972	Cincinnati	**154**	**645**	107	**198**	31	11	6	57	10	.307
1973	Cincinnati	160	**680**	115	**230**	36	8	5	64	10	**.338**
1974	Cincinnati	**163**	652	**110**	185	**45**	7	3	51	2	.284
1975	Cincinnati	**162**	662	**112**	210	**47**	4	7	74	0	.317
1976	Cincinnati	162	665	**130**	**215**	**42**	6	10	63	9	.323
1977	Cincinnati	**162**	**655**	95	204	38	7	9	64	16	.311
1978	Cincinnati	159	655	103	198	**51**	3	7	52	13	.302
1979	Philadelphia	163	628	90	208	40	5	4	59	20	.331
1980	Philadelphia	162	655	95	185	**42**	1	1	64	12	.282
1981	Philadelphia	107	431	73	**140**	18	5	0	33	4	.325
1982	Philadelphia	162	634	80	172	25	4	3	54	8	.271
1983	Philadelphia	151	493	52	121	14	3	0	45	7	.245
1984	Montreal	95	278	34	72	6	2	0	23	1	.259
1984	Cincinnati	26	96	9	35	9	0	0	11	0	.365
1985	Cincinnati	119	405	60	107	12	2	2	46	8	.264
1986	Cincinnati	72	237	15	52	8	2	0	25	3	.219
Totals		3562	14053	2165	4256	746	135	160	1314	198	.303

Bold = Led league

Notes
>17-time All-Star selection (1965, 1967–1971, 1973–1982, 1985);
>Played in 14 postseason series, including six World Series in which he hit .269 in 130 at-bats with 2 home runs and 9 RBI, and was 1975 World Series MVP with a .370 average in 27 at-bats;
>National League Rookie of the Year (1963) and National League MVP (1973);
>Career leader in games, at-bats, and hits;
>Only player to play at least 600 games at four different positions (left field 671; first base 939; third base 634; second base 628), and won 2 outfield Gold Gloves.

Babe Ruth (for more information, see pages 52-53)

Year	Team	G	AB	R	H	2B	3B	HR	RBI	SB	AVG
1914	Boston	5	10	1	2	1	0	0	2	0	.200
1915	Boston	42	92	16	29	10	1	4	21	0	.315
1916	Boston	67	136	18	37	5	3	3	15	0	.272
1917	Boston	52	123	14	40	6	3	2	12	0	.325
1918	Boston	95	317	50	95	26	11	**11**	66	6	.300
1919	Boston	130	432	**103**	139	34	12	**29**	**114**	7	.322
1920	N.Y. Yankees	142	458	**158**	172	36	9	**54**	**137**	14	.376
1921	N.Y. Yankees	152	540	**177**	204	44	16	**59**	**171**	17	.378
1922	N.Y. Yankees	110	406	94	128	24	8	35	99	2	.315
1923	N.Y. Yankees	152	522	**151**	205	45	13	**41**	**131**	17	.393
1924	N.Y. Yankees	153	529	**143**	200	39	7	**46**	121	9	**.378**
1925	N.Y. Yankees	98	359	61	104	12	2	25	66	2	.290
1926	N.Y. Yankees	152	495	**139**	184	30	5	**47**	**146**	11	.372
1927	N.Y. Yankees	151	540	**158**	192	29	8	**60**	164	7	.356
1928	N.Y. Yankees	154	536	**163**	173	29	8	**54**	**142**	4	.323
1929	N.Y. Yankees	135	499	121	172	26	6	**46**	154	5	.345
1930	N.Y. Yankees	145	518	150	186	28	9	**49**	153	10	.359
1931	N.Y. Yankees	145	534	149	199	31	3	**46**	163	5	.373
1932	N.Y. Yankees	133	457	120	156	13	5	41	137	2	.341
1933	N.Y. Yankees	137	459	97	138	21	3	34	103	4	.301
1934	N.Y. Yankees	125	365	78	105	17	4	22	84	1	.288
1935	Boston Braves	28	72	13	13	0	0	6	12	0	.181
Totals		2503	8399	2174	2873	506	136	714	2213	123	.342

Bold = Led league

Notes

>One of five charter members elected to the Hall of Fame (1936);

>In 1933, hit first homer in All-Star Game history;

>Participated in 10 World Series (1915, 1916, 1918, 1921–1923, 1926–1928, 1932), hitting .326 with 15 home runs in 129 at-bats, including a record two 3-homer games, and pitched in three games, posting a 3–0 record and 0.87 ERA in 31 innings;

>Ranks in the top ten in: slugging percentage (.690, first), on-base percentage (.474), homers, RBI (second), walks, runs (both third), and batting average (tenth);

>Broke the single-season home run record four times (1919, 1920, 1921, and 1927);

>Was a pitcher until 1918, before pitching and playing the outfield in 1918–1919 and being moved to the outfield in 1920, posting a 94–46 record and 2.28 ERA.

Mike Schmidt (for more information, see pages 54-55)

Year	Team	G	AB	R	H	2B	3B	HR	RBI	SB	AVG
1972	Philadelphia	13	34	2	7	0	0	1	3	0	.206
1973	Philadelphia	132	367	43	72	11	0	18	52	8	.196
1974	Philadelphia	162	568	108	160	28	7	**36**	116	23	.282
1975	Philadelphia	158	562	93	140	34	3	**38**	95	29	.249
1976	Philadelphia	160	584	112	153	31	4	**38**	107	14	.262
1977	Philadelphia	154	544	114	149	27	11	38	101	15	.274
1978	Philadelphia	145	513	93	129	27	2	21	78	19	.251
1979	Philadelphia	160	541	109	137	25	4	45	114	9	.253
1980	Philadelphia	150	548	104	157	25	8	**48**	**121**	12	.286
1981	Philadelphia	102	354	**78**	112	19	2	**31**	**91**	12	.316
1982	Philadelphia	148	514	108	144	26	3	35	87	14	.280
1983	Philadelphia	154	534	104	136	16	4	**40**	109	7	.255
1984	Philadelphia	151	528	93	146	23	3	**36**	**106**	5	.277
1985	Philadelphia	158	549	89	152	31	5	33	93	1	.277
1986	Philadelphia	160	552	97	160	29	1	**37**	**119**	1	.290
1987	Philadelphia	147	522	88	153	28	0	35	113	2	.293
1988	Philadelphia	108	390	52	97	21	2	12	62	3	.249
1989	Philadelphia	42	148	19	30	7	0	6	28	0	.203
Totals		2404	8352	1506	2234	408	59	548	1595	174	.267

Bold = Led league

Notes

>First-ballot Hall of Fame inductee (1995);

>Selected to 12 All-Star teams (1974, 1976, 1977, 1979–1984, 1986, 1987, 1989). He retired in May 1989, and although he was still voted the starting third baseman by the fans as a tribute to his career, Schmidt did not play in the 1989 game;

>Participated in eight postseason series, including two World Series (1980, 1983), hitting .220 with 2 home runs in 41 at-bats, and was 1980 World Series MVP;

>Three-time National League MVP (1980, 1981, 1986);

>10-time National League Gold Glove winner at third base (1976–1984, 1986);

>Owns record for most career home runs by a third baseman;

>Established record for most seasons leading National League in homers (eight);

>Led the league in strikeouts four times, including three times in his first four full seasons, but developed a good eye and led the league in walks four times, too;

>Hit 4 home runs in a game (April 7, 1976, at Chicago);

>One of four players (Barry Bonds, Roy Campanella, and Stan Musial) to win the National League MVP award at least three times.

Alfonso Soriano (for more information, see pages 94-95)

Year	Team	G	AB	R	H	2B	3B	HR	RBI	SB	AVG
1999	N.Y. Yankees	9	8	2	1	0	0	1	1	0	.125
2000	N.Y. Yankees	22	50	5	9	3	0	2	3	2	.180
2001	N.Y. Yankees	158	574	77	154	34	3	18	73	43	.268
2002	N.Y. Yankees	156	**696**	**128**	**209**	51	2	39	102	**41**	.300
2003	N.Y. Yankees	156	**682**	114	198	36	5	38	91	35	.290
Totals		501	2010	326	571	124	10	98	270	121	.284

Bold = Led league

Notes
>Two-time All Star (2002, 2003);
>Played in three postseason series, including two World Series (2001, 2003), in which he hit .234 with 2 home runs and 4 RBI in 47 at-bats;
>Hit a 2-run "walk-off" home run to defeat Seattle in Game Four of the 2001 ALCS, becoming the first rookie in history to hit a walk-off postseason homer;
>Sixth player, and only second American Leaguer, to post consecutive 30 homer-30 steal seasons;
>Only one rookie has matched or exceeded Soriano's 18 home runs and 43 stolen bases (Tommie Agee, 22 homers and 44 steals in 1966);
>Established single-season record with 13 leadoff home runs (2003);
>One of three players to combine to hit at least 50 homers and steal 50 bases during the 2002–2003 seasons (joining Carlos Beltran and Aaron Boone);
>In 2003, led league in at-bats (first), and ranked among league leaders in steals (fourth), home runs (tied for fifth), extra-base hits (sixth), and runs (sixth);
>In 2002, led American League in extra-base hits, at-bats, runs, hits, and steals, and among league leaders in doubles (third), homers (fifth), and slugging percentage (ninth);
>In 2000, played 10 games at third base, nine at shortstop, and just one game at second base, but began 2001 as the opening day second baseman;
>Born in Dominican Republic, and played two minor league seasons in Japan, one season in Japan's major leagues, and then retired from Japanese baseball and was declared a free agent before signing with Yankees on September 29, 1998.

Sammy Sosa (for more information, see pages 56-57)

Year	Team	G	AB	R	H	2B	3B	HR	RBI	SB	AVG
1989	Texas	25	84	8	20	3	0	1	3	0	.238
1989	Chi. White Sox	33	99	19	27	5	0	3	10	7	.273
1990	Chi. White Sox	153	532	72	124	26	10	15	70	32	.233
1991	Chi. White Sox	116	316	39	64	10	1	10	33	13	.203
1992	Chicago Cubs	67	262	41	68	7	2	8	25	15	.260
1993	Chicago Cubs	159	598	92	156	25	5	33	93	36	.261
1994	Chicago Cubs	105	426	59	128	17	6	25	70	22	.300
1995	Chicago Cubs	**144**	564	89	151	17	3	36	119	34	.268
1996	Chicago Cubs	124	498	84	136	21	2	40	100	18	.273
1997	Chicago Cubs	**162**	642	90	161	31	4	36	119	22	.251
1998	Chicago Cubs	159	643	**134**	198	20	0	66	**158**	18	.308
1999	Chicago Cubs	**162**	625	114	180	24	2	63	141	7	.288
2000	Chicago Cubs	156	604	106	193	38	1	**50**	138	7	.320
2001	Chicago Cubs	160	577	**146**	189	34	5	64	**160**	0	.328
2002	Chicago Cubs	150	556	**122**	160	19	2	**49**	108	2	.288
2003	Chicago Cubs	137	517	99	144	22	0	40	103	0	.279
Totals		2012	7543	1314	2099	319	43	539	1450	233	.278

Bold = Led league

Notes
>Selected to six All-Star Games (1995, 1998–2002);
>Played in two postseason series, hitting .245 with 2 homers in 53 at-bats;
>National League Most Valuable Player award winner (1998);
>Only player in major-league history to have three 60-homer seasons;
>Joined Babe Ruth and Mark McGwire as the only players with more than two 50-homer seasons in their career (all have hit at least 50 home runs four times);
>Finished first or second in the National League in home runs five consecutive seasons (1998–2002);
>First player in National League history to hit at least 40 home runs in six consecutive seasons (1998–2003) and first player in National League history with nine consecutive 100-RBI seasons (1995–2003);
>Ranks tenth on the all-time home run list (539);
>On August 10, 2002, became the second player in history to hit 3 three-run homers in the same game (Walker Cooper on July 6, 1949).

Ichiro Suzuki (for more information, see pages 96-97)

Year	Team	G	AB	R	H	2B	3B	HR	RBI	SB	AVG
2001	Seattle	157	**692**	127	**242**	34	8	8	69	**56**	.350
2002	Seattle	157	647	111	208	27	8	8	51	31	.321
2003	Seattle	159	679	111	212	29	8	13	62	34	.312
Totals		473	2018	349	662	90	24	29	182	121	.328

Bold = Led league

Notes

>Three-time All Star (2001–2003), led the majors in All-Star balloting all three seasons, and was only the sixth rookie to start an All-Star Game, and the first rookie outfielder to start since Tony Oliva in 1964;

>Played in two postseason series, hitting .421 in 38 at-bats with 3 stolen bases;

>American League Most Valuable Player and Rookie of the Year (2001), becoming only the second player to win both awards in the same season (Fred Lynn, 1975);

>American League Gold Glove outfielder (2001–2003);

>Set major-league record for most hits in first two seasons (450);

>Led majors in infield hits in 2002 (54);

>In 2001, first player since Jackie Robinson in 1949 to lead majors in batting average and stolen bases in the same season;

>Was second rookie ever to lead league in average (Tony Oliva, 1964);

>Established American League rookie records for at-bats (692) and hits (242);

>His 242 hits in 2001 were the most by a player in a season since 1930 (Bill Terry, Chuck Klein);

>In 2001, first major league player with three hitting streaks of 15 or more games since Cecil Cooper in 1980;

>Played nine years in Japan prior to joining Seattle;

>First Japanese position player to sign with a Major League club (November 2000);

>Three-time Most Valuable Player in Japan, was selected to their "Best Nine" seven consecutive years, and won seven consecutive batting titles and Gold Glove awards.

Jim Thome (for more information, see pages 58-59)

Year	Team	G	AB	R	H	2B	3B	HR	RBI	SB	AVG
1991	Cleveland	27	98	7	25	4	2	1	9	1	.255
1992	Cleveland	40	117	8	24	3	1	2	12	2	.205
1993	Cleveland	47	154	28	41	11	0	7	22	2	.266
1994	Cleveland	98	321	58	86	20	1	20	52	3	.268
1995	Cleveland	137	452	92	142	29	3	25	73	4	.314
1996	Cleveland	151	505	122	157	28	5	38	116	2	.311
1997	Cleveland	147	496	104	142	25	0	40	102	1	.286
1998	Cleveland	123	440	89	129	34	2	30	85	1	.293
1999	Cleveland	146	494	101	137	27	2	33	108	0	.277
2000	Cleveland	158	557	106	150	33	1	37	106	1	.269
2001	Cleveland	156	526	101	153	26	1	49	124	0	.291
2002	Cleveland	147	480	101	146	19	2	52	118	1	.304
2003	Philadelphia	159	578	111	154	30	3	**47**	131	0	.266
Totals		1536	5218	1028	1486	289	23	381	1058	18	.285

Bold = Led league

Notes
>Selected to three All-Star Games (1997–1999);
>Played in 11 postseason series, including two World Series (1995, 1997) in which he hit .255 with 3 home runs and 6 RBI in 47 at-bats;
>In his first season in the National League, established a career high in RBI (131) and broke Phillies' club-record for homers by a left-hander hitter (Chuck Klein had 43 in 1929);
>Finished second in the majors in homers in 2002, and tied for Major League lead in home runs in 2003;
>Homered in seven consecutive games (June 25–July 3, 2002), one game shy of the Major League record;
>Owns Indians single-season (52 in 2002) and career (334) home run records;
>Played third base for six seasons (1991–1996) before moving to first base in 1997;
>Played baseball and basketball at Illinois Central College.

Honus Wagner (for more information, see pages 98-99)

Year	Team	G	AB	R	H	2B	3B	HR	RBI	SB	AVG
1897	Louisville	61	237	37	80	17	4	2	39	19	.338
1898	Louisville	151	588	80	176	29	3	10	105	27	.299
1899	Louisville	147	571	98	192	43	13	7	113	37	.336
1900	Pittsburgh	135	527	107	201	**45**	**22**	4	100	38	**.381**
1901	Pittsburgh	140	549	101	194	37	11	6	**126**	**49**	.353
1902	Pittsburgh	136	534	**105**	176	**30**	16	3	**91**	**42**	.330
1903	Pittsburgh	129	512	97	182	30	**19**	5	101	46	**.355**
1904	Pittsburgh	132	490	97	171	**44**	14	4	75	**53**	**.349**
1905	Pittsburgh	147	548	114	199	32	14	6	101	57	.363
1906	Pittsburgh	142	516	**103**	175	**38**	9	2	71	53	**.339**
1907	Pittsburgh	142	515	98	180	**38**	14	6	82	**61**	**.350**
1908	Pittsburgh	151	568	100	**201**	**39**	**19**	10	**109**	53	**.354**
1909	Pittsburgh	137	495	92	168	**39**	10	5	**100**	35	**.339**
1910	Pittsburgh	150	556	90	**178**	34	8	4	81	24	.320
1911	Pittsburgh	130	473	87	158	23	16	9	89	20	**.334**
1912	Pittsburgh	145	558	91	181	35	20	7	**102**	26	.324
1913	Pittsburgh	114	413	51	124	18	4	3	56	21	.300
1914	Pittsburgh	150	552	60	139	15	9	1	50	23	.252
1915	Pittsburgh	156	566	68	155	32	17	6	78	22	.274
1916	Pittsburgh	123	432	45	124	15	9	1	39	11	.287
1917	Pittsburgh	74	230	15	61	7	1	0	24	5	.265
Totals		2792	10430	1736	3415	640	252	101	1732	722	.327

Bold = Led league

Notes

>One of five charter members of the Hall of Fame (1936);

>Played in two World Series (1903, 1909), hitting .275 with 9 RBI and 9 steals in 51 at-bats;

>Ranks in the all-time top ten in: triples (third), hits (eighth), doubles (eighth), and stolen bases (tenth);

>Tied with Tony Gwynn for most National League batting average titles (eight);

>Nominated by John McGraw, Branch Rickey, and other highly-regarded contemporaries as the best player they ever saw, even better than Babe Ruth;

Ted Williams (for more information, see pages 112-113)

Year	Team	G	AB	R	H	2B	3B	HR	RBI	SB	AVG
1939	Boston	149	565	131	185	44	11	31	**145**	2	.327
1940	Boston	144	561	**134**	193	43	14	23	113	4	.344
1941	Boston	143	456	**135**	185	33	3	**37**	120	2	**.406**
1942	Boston	150	522	**141**	186	34	5	**36**	**137**	3	**.356**
1946	Boston	150	514	**142**	176	37	8	38	123	0	.342
1947	Boston	156	528	**125**	181	40	9	**32**	**114**	0	**.343**
1948	Boston	137	509	124	188	**44**	3	25	127	4	**.369**
1949	Boston	**155**	566	**150**	194	**39**	3	**43**	**159**	1	.343
1950	Boston	89	334	82	106	24	1	28	97	3	.317
1951	Boston	148	531	109	169	28	4	30	126	1	.318
1952	Boston	6	10	2	4	0	1	1	3	0	.400
1953	Boston	37	91	17	37	6	0	13	34	0	.407
1954	Boston	117	386	93	133	23	1	29	89	0	.345
1955	Boston	98	320	77	114	21	3	28	83	2	.356
1956	Boston	136	400	71	138	28	2	24	82	0	.345
1957	Boston	132	420	96	163	28	1	38	87	0	**.388**
1958	Boston	129	411	81	135	23	2	26	85	1	**.328**
1959	Boston	103	272	32	69	15	0	10	43	0	.254
1960	Boston	113	310	56	98	15	0	29	72	1	.316
Totals		2292	7706	1798	2654	525	71	521	1839	24	.344

Bold = Led league

Notes
>First-ballot Hall of Fame inductee (1966);
>Played in 18 All-Star Games (1940–1942, 1946–1951, 1953–1960);
>Participated in one World Series (1946), hitting .200 with 1 RBI in 25 at-bats;
>Two-time American League MVP (1946, 1949), and finished in the top 10 in voting 12 times;
>Joined Rogers Hornsby as only players with multiple Triple Crowns (1942, 1947);
>Ranks in the top ten of numerous categories: on-base percentage (.482, first), slugging percentage (.634, second), walks (fourth), and batting average (seventh);
>Was hitting .39955 (or .400) entering the final day of the 1941 season. Williams refused to sit on his average, and he went 6-for-8 in the doubleheader to hit .406 and be the last .400 hitter in the majors;
>Hit .388 at age 39, including a .453 average in the second half of the 1957 season;
>Missed nearly five seasons because he served as a pilot in World War II (1943–1945) and the Korean War (1952–1953).

Hack Wilson (for more information, see pages 82-83)

Year	Team	G	AB	R	H	2B	3B	HR	RBI	SB	AVG
1923	N.Y. Giants	3	10	0	2	0	0	0	0	0	.200
1924	N.Y. Giants	107	383	62	113	19	12	10	57	4	.295
1925	N.Y. Giants	62	180	28	43	7	4	6	30	5	.239
1926	Chicago Cubs	142	529	97	170	36	8	**21**	109	10	.321
1927	Chicago Cubs	146	551	119	175	30	12	**30**	129	13	.318
1928	Chicago Cubs	145	520	89	163	32	9	**31**	120	4	.313
1929	Chicago Cubs	150	574	135	198	30	5	39	**159**	3	.345
1930	Chicago Cubs	155	585	146	208	35	6	**56**	**191**	3	.356
1931	Chicago Cubs	112	395	66	103	22	4	13	61	1	.261
1932	Brooklyn	135	481	77	143	37	5	23	123	2	.297
1933	Brooklyn	117	360	41	96	13	2	9	54	7	.267
1934	Brooklyn	67	172	24	45	5	0	6	27	0	.262
1934	Philadelphia	7	20	0	2	0	0	0	3	0	.100
Totals		1348	4760	884	1461	266	67	244	1063	52	.307

Bold = Led league

Notes
>Inducted into Hall of Fame (1979);
>Played in two World Series (1924, 1929), hitting .319 with 3 RBI in 47 at-bats;
>Owns major league record for RBI in a season (191 in 1930);
>His 56 home runs in 1930 stood as a National League record for 68 years until broken by Mark McGwire and Sammy Sosa in 1998;
>Of modern era players, Wilson physically resembled former Minnesota Twins star Kirby Puckett. He stood just 5-feet, 6-inches tall, with large shoulders and chest, thick legs, and small (size 6) feet, but played a solid center field and once led the league in putouts;
>Built his strength as a youth by working in a locomotive factory and swinging a sledge hammer.

Carl Yastrezemski (for more information, see pages 114-115)

Year	Team	G	AB	R	H	2B	3B	HR	RBI	SB	AVG
1961	Boston	148	583	71	155	31	6	11	80	6	.266
1962	Boston	160	646	99	191	43	6	19	94	7	.296
1963	Boston	151	570	91	**183**	**40**	3	14	68	8	**.321**
1964	Boston	151	567	77	164	29	9	15	67	6	.289
1965	Boston	133	494	78	154	**45**	3	20	72	7	.312
1966	Boston	160	594	81	165	**39**	2	16	80	8	.278
1967	Boston	161	579	**112**	**189**	31	4	**44**	**121**	10	**.326**
1968	Boston	157	539	90	162	32	2	23	74	13	**.301**
1969	Boston	**162**	603	96	154	28	2	40	111	15	.255
1970	Boston	161	566	**125**	186	29	0	40	102	23	.329
1971	Boston	148	508	75	129	21	2	15	70	8	.254
1972	Boston	125	455	70	120	18	2	12	68	5	.264
1973	Boston	152	540	82	160	25	4	19	95	9	.296
1974	Boston	148	515	**93**	155	25	2	15	79	12	.301
1975	Boston	149	543	91	146	30	1	14	60	8	.269
1976	Boston	155	546	71	146	23	2	21	102	5	.267
1977	Boston	150	558	99	165	27	3	28	102	11	.296
1978	Boston	144	523	70	145	21	2	17	81	4	.277
1979	Boston	147	518	69	140	28	1	21	87	3	.270
1980	Boston	105	364	49	100	21	1	15	50	0	.275
1981	Boston	91	338	36	83	14	1	7	53	0	.246
1982	Boston	131	459	53	126	22	1	16	72	0	.275
1983	Boston	119	380	38	101	24	0	10	56	0	.266
Totals		3308	11988	1816	3419	646	59	452	1844	168	.285

Bold = Led league

Notes

>First-ballot Hall of Fame inductee (1989);
>Participated in 18 All-Star Games (1963, 1965–1979, 1982, 1983);
>Played in two World Series (1967, 1975), hitting .352 with 3 homers in 54 at-bats;
>American League MVP (1967), when he won the Triple Crown;
>Won seven American League Gold Glove awards as an outfielder;
>Ranks in the top ten in: games played (second), at-bats (third), hits (sixth), walks (sixth), and doubles (seventh);
>Last name pronounced yuhz-STREM-ski, but almost always referred to as "Yaz";
>Was Ted Williams' replacement in left field, which means the Red Sox had a Hall of Fame left fielder in their lineup for 45 consecutive years.

Photo Credits

All player head shots are courtesy of and copyright © MLB Photos except: Corbis: 32, 35, 42, 67, 82, 103, 111.

Action photos: AP/Wide World: 15, 38, Corbis: 44, 66, 102, 110; National Baseball Library: 98; Transcendental Graphics: 26. All other action photos are courtesy of and copyright © MLB Photos, with the following by these specific photographers: David Durochick: 57; Allen Kee: 40; Brad Mangin: 80; Rich Pilling: 8, 10, 21, 46, 55, 73, 91, 94, 97, 114; John Reid III: 19, 51; Russell Skeoch: 17; Don Smith: 37; Tony Tomsic: 12; John Williamson: 48, 63; Michael Zagaris: 29, 68.

Acknowledgments

All statistical information in this book was gathered from official Major League Baseball sources, including www.mlb.com, the Elias Sport Bureau, and individual team Web sites. Thanks to Eric Enders for casting his expert eye on the final draft. Thanks also to Rich Pilling and Paul Cunningham of MLB Photos.

Trivia Answers

(Page: answer) 9: chicken; 11: Twins and Angels; San Juan; 14: Vince and Dom; 16: French; 18: 1984 and 1998; 20: New York Mets; 23: Browns; 25: Carlton Fisk; 26: Busch Stadium; 28: Boston Red Sox; 33: Milwaukee; 34: It had no lights; 36: Pittsburgh Pirates; 39: the 1935 Pittsburgh Crawfords; 41: Cincinnati Reds; 42: "Reggie" candy bar; 45: New York and San Francisco; 47: Sammy Sosa; 49: Washington Senators; 50: Roger Maris; 53: Boston Red Sox; 54: Baltimore Orioles; 55: Wrigley Field; 59: Florida Marlins; 62: Houston Astrodome; 65: "Big Red Machine"; 67: Yogi Bear; 69: 1977; 71: It's "Ramon" backward!; 72: "Bronx Bombers"; 74: Sammy Sosa; 76: 1984; 79: Anaheim Angels; 81: Green Monster; 82: Lou Gehrig, 184 in 1930; 86: 1964 and 1967; 88: "The Georgia Peach"; 90: 1990; 93: Ebbets Field; 95: 12; 96: Jose Canseco, Alex Rodriguez, and Barry Bonds; 98: 1909; 102: Connie Mack; 104: "The Iron Horse"; 107: Joe Morgan; 108: Eddie Murray; 111: Frank hit a home run!; 113: Ted hit a home run!; 115: Brooks Robinson.

About the Authors

James Buckley, Jr., has written more than 25 books about baseball, including *Eyewitness Baseball, The Visual Dictionary of Baseball,* and *Play Ball: The Official Major League Guide for Young Players.*

Matt Marini is a freelance writer in Los Angeles with more than a decade of experience in compiling and working with professional sports statistics.